גימטריה

עזר

GEMATRIA AZER
A Taste Of Torah From Exodus

Dr. Akiva Gamliel Belk

Dean of Jewish Studies at
B'nai Noach Torah Institute, LLC

Copyright © 2014 Dr. Akiva Gamliel Belk

All rights reserved

ISBN-10: 0615984983

ISBN -13: 978-0615984988

Publisher
B'nai Noach Torah Institute, LLC,
Post Office Box 14
Cedar Hill, Missouri 63016
First Edition 2014

DEDICATED

Azer
By Dr. Akiva Gamliel Belk

Azer means helper, partner or teammate,
I am your partner and you are mine, great!

Partners are colleagues, associates, coworkers,
husband or wife who are not loafers or shirkers!

Between mates a special relationship is shared,
Both the Husband and the Wife are paired.

Challenges come and heartaches too,
So lean on each other and God to get through.

Distress, grief, pain is too much to face alone,
Husband and wife share bone of bone.

Reach out and touch that very special one,
Your special partner for all they have done.

Remember all that you share
with love and tenderness and care...

FORWARD

Writing a book is a MONUMENTAL project. I know!! My husband, Dr. Akiva Gamliel is the author of more than a dozen books as noted in the last pages of this book. His passion is to help others. He is a generous man who shares what he learns. He is an inspired writer. Many nights my husband is awakened by the Creator of the Universe. He softly says to me as he arises, 'I can't sleep. I need to study for awhile.' He then arises to study and record inspirations. He may write for hours not wanting to miss any part of these revelations.

Dr Akiva Gamliel is an explorer... an investigator... a detective of Torah study... a miner of Gematria and a student of God's Holy Word. He is willing to sacrifice to study, and to study to discover Gematrias Gems to share with us. He is a willing receptacle. When the Creator wants knowledge disseminated He can use any vessel willing to be the conduit. In our prayers we say, '...He who removes sleep from our eyelids...' There are many dedicated individuals our

Creator uses. There could me more if we were willing to give up nights of sleep, and other things important to us just for Torah study! Dr. Akiva Gamliel Belk writes for hours at a time oblivious to whatever else is going on around him. He, so to speak, closes the doors and windows around him to enter this time of study and writing.

I have read all of my husbands books and have found each of them to be filled with great Torah insights and wisdom. This book, *Gematria Azer, A Taste of Torah from Exodus* is a springboard to Torah Study and is easily understood. One can go to any depth they want in utilizing this Torah Study tool.

Studying with my husband is an adventure. One never knows what thrill is around the next curve or what exciting point he is building up to until you are there.

Rebbetzin Revi Belk
Dean of Ladies Studies
B'nai Noach Torah Institute, LLC

PREFACE

It very important to write a book that can fill hearts with Ha Torah and that can lend a hand in improving our relationship with our Creator Ha Torah is alive for all to learn, to follow and to enjoy. Only Ha Torah has the power to restore the weak and damaged parts of our lives . As an author, my goal and joy in writing each book is to help others desiring to know more about God and learn of His Glorious Beauty and Wonders. It gives me great joy to share lessons from the Gematria of Ha Torah. It is exciting to learn while at the same time share a few Words to lift and encourage others along life's path. Can there be a greater reward?

Each chapter is from the Weekly Parshat which dates back thousands of years. We, the Jewish People, were carried off into captivity to Babylon. Our Temple was destroyed. Our Holy items desecrated! The Holy City of Jerusalem lay in ruins. The Holy Land was occupied by invading armies. It was during these most trying times Sages like Daniel and Mordicai divided the Torah

Portion of the Bible into study sections. We followed their guidance. We began the practice of reading these portions known as the Weekly Parsha / Parshat of Ha Torah each Sabbath when we gathered for morning prayers. This became a custom for us that is now thousands of years old. The writings in this book follow the ancient tradition of Bible Study established for our benefit. Down through the centuries this has become the foundation of Torah Study for Jewish People worldwide.

Each chapter in this book is from the Weekly Parshat of the Book of Shemot / Exodus. I invite you to join with me in this wonderful and exciting method of learning The Word of The Lord God. May all who study His Words be blessed!!

What Is Gematria?

The word Gematria is a Greek word that comes from geometry which is a branch of mathematics. It is important to understand this is how the people of the world view Gematria. The world thinks of Hebrew Letters and numbers like they think of letters and numbers of their own language. The reason for this is because the world views Gematria through the eyes of geometry. This makes sense to the world. And those of us who are Jewish can see how and why the world views Gematria from this position. HOWEVER, and I MUST emphasize, this is a huge HOWEVER, Gematria is not the correct term for understanding The Letters, and Numbers of Hebrew. The correct term is ???? Oht meaning 'A Sign, A marvel, A Symbol... Yet even ???? Oht does not express the entire meaning. Hebrew Letters and Numbers are also a Mystical form of revelation. Hebrew Letters and Numbers provide us with Spiritual revelation. Hebrew Letters and Numbers have the power of opening avenues that are new to us. Torah Codes have the power of prophecy. So, although I use the term

Gematria this term does not explain or reveal the true meaning or intent of the Spiritual Revelations hidden in Hebrew Letters and Numbers.

Hebrew is the original language of the universe. The Lord God Created the Universe with ten utterances spoken from the Hebrew language. Hebrew is separated from all other languages of the world. We call It Loshon Kodesh, the Holy Language. Within the pages of this book are Spiritual Revelations that can help us. One of the Revelations has to do with The Letter ת Tav. The Letter ת Tav is the last letter of the Word אות Oht Throughout Loshon Kodesh the Letter ת Tav Mystically appears as the first Letter of a Word which does not begin with The Letter Tav. This is a Mystical Phenomena that cannot be translated into any other language. This Mystical Phenomena is exclusive to The Words of Ha Torah. Our Creator Instructed Moshe to place The Letter Tav in front of certain HEBREW WORDS that He Desired to change the Numerical Calculation on and to Give the reader a Sign. The purpose for Giving a Sign is to indicate that this is a good place to spend time studying. There is a hidden Revelation here. Geometry and mathematical calculations and translations do not reveal what is in Loshon Kodesh! Only experienced individuals who have walked these paths look for these special Mystical signs in the Hebrew Text of The Hebrew Scriptures. This is only one example of the many signs within Loshon Kodesh.

Lets say for example that the Word emphasized in Hebrew in The Torah by The Letter Tav was לָמֹד meaning to learn. The Word לָמֹד Law Mohd would become תִלְמַד Tee Lih Mad which still means to learn. The Gematria relationship would change from being 74 to 474.

לָמֹד	תִלְמַד
Law Mohd / To Learn	Tee Lih Mad / To Learn
74 = 4ד 40מ 30ל	474 = 4ד 40מ 30ל 400ת

The meaning which is translated does not change. However the Mystical revelation changes. There is NO WAY for other languages to reflect the Mysticism in the translation. Lets say that we still wanted to try to reflect the

Mysticism into the English language. Let's say we chose the Letter Z to do this. Now where would we place the Letter Z. Would we write z-to learn or to z-learn? Then if one were to do this how would they mine in the English language for the hidden revelation? How would they explore in English? The point is that the revelation is hidden among the Letters and numerical Revelations within Hebrew. It is possible to translate what is hidden into English. Dear Ones, a great deal of diligent research is necessary to learn Torah Truths and to find answers and to receive revelations... Hebrew Letters and Numbers are a Sign and contain many revelations. Gematria is only a small portion of what is hidden in the Letters, Numbers, Words, Phrases, etc., of The Hebrew Language. Hebrew Letters and Numbers are NOT numerology!! Hebrew Letters and Numbers are NOT geometry!! Please do not be fooled by all the discussions trying to broaden the boundaries of what The Lord God ONLY Established just among The Hebrew Letters and Numbers!!There are untold thousands upon thousands of Revelations hidden within the Letters and Numbers of Hebrew that translators are entirely oblivious too. These are the Revelations I try to share in the discussions in this book. This is why they are call Mysterious signs or Mystical revelations... They are NOT magical! The Revelations are Holy and Spiritual. The Hidden Revelations have great potential not understood by the human mind...

To better understand and to view the Hebrew Letters and Numbers please refer to the Gematria Chart at the conclusion of the book.

ACKNOWLEDGMENTS

Oh Creator of the Universe, thank You for this opportunity to share the Gematrias in this book. Thank You for forgiving us of our every sin. Thank You for helping us to return to Torah Observances. Thank You for daily assisting us with efforts to improve. Thank You for every blessing. Thank you for the bread of life. Thank you for Revi... Kaw Naw Nah Haw Raw.

My wife, Revi is a soft spoken, quite, tiny lady, in physical stature, but very big in showing others love, kindness, patience and Observing Torah Mitzvot. Brachah Rivkah is a courageous soul. I love you Revi and thank our Creator for every breath He Has Given Us! Kaw Naw Nah Haw Raw. Revi thank you for assisting greatly with the editing and formatting of this book. I greatly appreciate your every effort!

Thank you Oh God our Creator and Momma Daddy for giving me the breath of life.

GEMATRIA AZER

A Taste Of Torah From Exodus

Table of Contents

DEDICATED	5
FORWARD	7
PREFACE	9
What Is Gematria?	11
ACKNOWLEDGMENTS	17
Parshat Shemot Shemot	21
Exodus 1.1 - 6.1	21
Parshat Shemot Va'eira	31
Exodus 6.2 - 9.35	31
Parshat Shemot Va'eira	47
Exodus 10.1 - 13.16	47
Parshat Shemot Beshalach	57
Exodus 13.17 - 17.16	57
Parshat Shemot Yitro	67
Exodus 18.1 - 20.23	67
Parshat Shemot Mishpatim	83
Exodus 21.1 - 24.18	83

Parshat Shemot Terumah..................................91
   Exodus 25.1 - 27:19...91
Parshat Shemot Tezaveh..................................97
   Exodus 27:20 - 30.10.......................................97
Parshat Shemot Ki TeeSaw............................105
   Exodus 30:11 - 34.35.....................................105
Parshat Shemot Vayakhel...............................115
   Exodus 35.1 - 38.20.......................................115
Devri Torah Parshat Pekudei..........................129
   Shemot 38.21 - 40.38....................................129
SCRIPTURE INDEX..143
GEMATRIA INDEX..146
About The Author...149
Books By Dr. Akiva Gamliel............................153

Parshat Shemot Shemot

Exodus 1.1 - 6.1

How Do We Praise The Lord God?

Shemot 4.22

וְאָמַרְתָּ אֶל־פַּרְעֹה כֹּה אָמַר יְהוָה בְּנִי בְכֹרִי יִשְׂרָאֵל:

Exodus 4.22
And you will say to Pharaoh, Here is what The Lord Said, 'Yisroel is My firstborn son.'

Please explain what is meant by what The Lord Said, *'Yisroel is My firstborn son.'*

Who is Israel? Is Israel, Jacob? Is Israel all the descendants of Jacob? When The Lord God Says, Israel is my first born son what are the implications?

The Lord God is speaking ONLY of the People Israel. How do we know this?

Shemot 4.23

וָאֹמַר אֵלֶיךָ שַׁלַּח אֶת־בְּנִי וְיַעַבְדֵנִי וַתְּמָאֵן לְשַׁלְּחוֹ הִנֵּה אָנֹכִי הֹרֵג אֶת־בִּנְךָ בְּכֹרֶךָ:

Exodus 4.23
And I say to you, Let everything from the Letter Aleph to the Letter Tav of My son go, and he will serve Me; and if you refuse to let him go, behold, I will slay everything from the Letter Aleph to the Letter Tav of your son, your firstborn.

Shemot 19.6

וְאַתֶּם תִּהְיוּ־לִי מַמְלֶכֶת כֹּהֲנִים וְגוֹי קָדוֹשׁ אֵלֶּה הַדְּבָרִים אֲשֶׁר תְּדַבֵּר אֶל־בְּנֵי יִשְׂרָאֵל:

Exodus 19.6
And you shall be to me a Kingdom of Priests and a Holy Nation.

We are to serve The Lord God. Our Creator Commanded Pharaoh to let us go, to release us.

Why? So that we may serve Him. How are we to serve Him? We are to serve Him as a Kingdom of Priests.

The Gematria of בְּנִי בְכֹרִי יִשְׂרָאֵל meaning my son, my firstborn, Yisroel is 835. The Gematria of תְהִלֹּת Praises is also 835.

בְּנִי בְכֹרִי יִשְׂרָאֵל
Bih Nee   Vih Coh Ree   Israel
my son, my firstborn, Israel
ב 2 נ 50 י 10   ב 2 כ 20 ר 200 י 10 = 294
י 10 ש 300 ר 200 א 1 ל 30 = 541
835 = 294 + 541

תְהִלֹּת
Tih Hee Loht / Praises
ת 400 ה 5 ל 30 ת 400 = 835

Leading up to the Amidah we pray,

Shemot 15.11

מִי־כָמֹכָה בָּאֵלִם יְהֹוָה מִי כָּמֹכָה נֶאְדָּר בַּקֹּדֶשׁ נוֹרָא תְהִלֹּת עֹשֵׂה פֶלֶא :

Exodus 15.11

Who is like you, O Lord, among the gods? who is like you, glorious in holiness, fearful in **praises,** *doing wonders?*

We continue by praying, With a new song the redeemed ones praised, Your Great Name at the seashore together all of them gave thanks acknowledged Your Sovereignty and said,

Exodus 15.18
The Lord shall reign forever and forever.

Then just before we pray the Amidah we say,

Tehillim 51.17

אֲדֹנָי שְׂפָתַי תִּפְתָּח וּפִי יַגִּיד **תְּהִלָּתֶךָ**

Psalms 51.17
Master open my lips that my mouth may declare Your **praise!**

Tehillim 145.21

תְּהִלַּת יְהוָה יְדַבֶּר־פִּי וִיבָרֵךְ כָּל־בָּשָׂר שֵׁם קָדְשׁוֹ לְעוֹלָם וָעֶד :

Psalms 145.21

My mouth shall speak praise of the Lord; and [lead] all flesh in blessing His Holy Name for ever and ever.

The responsibility of the Jewish people, i.e. Israel, the firstborn son is to speak with our mouth praise of The Lord. The responsibility of everyone else is to follow us, the Priests, in Blessing His Holy Name forever and ever.

Psalms 100.4

A Psalm of thanksgiving. Make a joyful noise to the Lord, all the earth. Serve the Lord with gladness; come before his presence with singing. Know that the Lord is God; it is He who Made us, and we belong to him; we are His people, and the sheep of His pasture. Enter into His gates with thanksgiving, and into His courts with praise; be thankful to Him, and bless His Name. For the Lord is Good; His Loving Kindness is everlasting; and His Faithfulness endures to all generations.

The Lord God Has Chosen the People of Israel

to offer praise to Him. Everything that has flesh is to bless His Name. Everyone that has breath is to bless His Name. What is the Name of The Lord?

The Word תְהִלַת Tih Hee Lot begins and ends with the Letter ת Tav [400]. This is a SIGN to us who are the People of Israel. The Letter Tav represents Truth, the last Letter of אמת Emet, is Tav meaning Truth. The Letter Tav also represents אבת Oht meaning sign. The Letters between תְהִלַת are representative of הֲלָה Hee Lawh meaning, Halo, Crown, Glory and Radiance. When we the People Yisroel Praise our King we become radiant. We glow. So in giving our praise to the Creator we Teach the World how to properly honor The Lord God.

Our praise of The Lord God is to be a dedicated, sanctified praise. Our praise is not merely an acknowledgment of the honor and worthiness of The Lord. We know The Lord God is Worthy to be praised. He is our Father. Our praise must be a Praise that is backed with substance!! This means we MUST be Holy! Our Praise MUST be founded on Holiness / Separation from the world. There is a great difference between dedicated praise from that which lack commitment... resolve... persistence...tenacity... great effort...

Ha Torah is Mystically showing us that there is a difference between dedicated zeal and enthusiasm from that of just zeal and enthusiasm. The People of Israel are chosen by The Lord God to be Holy.

Leviticus 11.45
For I am The Lord that Brings you out of the land of Egypt, to be your God; you shall therefore be Holy, for I Am Holy.

Ha Torah is Teaching us, the People of Israel, that we are separated! We are separated from those who were not delivered from slavery in Egypt by the Mighty Hand of God... We are separated from those who are not the Firstborn Son... We are separated from those whose soul did not stand at Mount Sinai and say 'we will do and we will hear'... We are separated from those who are not the Kingdom of Priests. We are separated from those who do NOT OBSERVE

THE SABBATH to keep it Holy... **We are separated from those who do not keep kosher... We are separated from those who do not observe the 613 Commands of Ha Torah...**

This is the substance that shows what the differences are between the People of Israel whose foundation requires dedicated zeal and enthusiasm from that of just zeal and enthusiasm and acknowledgments from the people of the world.

Dear Ones, the people of the world have not been where we have been. They have not experienced what we have experienced nor can they. This is what makes the difference in our foundation and their foundation. This is why we are the Priests who are called to lead the Praises of the people of the world to our Creator. This is why the People of Israel are radiant. The People of Israel meet each morning near dawn to offer / lead Praise to our Creator. The People of Israel meet each afternoon to offer / lead Praise to our Creator. The People of Israel meet each night as the sun sets to offer / lead praise to our Creator.

The People of Israel meet many, many special times throughout the year to offer / lead praise to our Creator. This is the substance... this is the dedication that radiates that glows that beams... between the beginning Tav and the ending Tav of תְּהִלַּת Tih Hee Lot, the honor of being My Son, My Firstborn, Yisroel.

The people of the world have a different view of us, the People of Israel. Their view is based much on what they have been taught by their Spiritual leaders. The Spiritual leaders are taught by their religious institutions. All of this is understandable. The same holds true for most of the People of Israel. For walls of misunderstanding to come down those who have helpful information that can fill in the gaps that can build bridges that share factual truthful information must do so. There is an educational process that MUST take place.

Trying to understand where people of other religions are and why they believe as they do should NOT be frightening to us. We should not be intimidated! It should NOT be wrong for us, the People our Creator Said are A Kingdom of Priests to reach out with helpful information. There is confusion in the world that we can help to clear up. We should do what we can. We should NOT sit back. Our purpose for reaching out to others must be understood. The people of the world must know our intentions are NOT to evangelize or convert those who are not Jewish.

Parshat Shemot Va'eira

Exodus 6.2 - 9.35

What Do We Really Need To Know?

Shemot 7.17

כֹּה אָמַר יְהוָֹה בְּזֹאת **תֵּדַע כִּי אֲנִי יְהוָֹה** הִנֵּה אָנֹכִי מַכֶּה ׀ בַּמַּטֶּה אֲשֶׁר־בְּיָדִי עַל־הַמַּיִם אֲשֶׁר בַּיְאֹר וְנֶהֶפְכוּ לְדָם:

Exodus 7.17
'...You will know that I am The Lord...'

Shemot 8.6

וַיֹּאמֶר לְמָחָר וַיֹּאמֶר כִּדְבָרְךָ לְמַעַן תֵּדַע כִּי־אֵין כַּיהוָֹה אֱלֹהֵינוּ:

Exodus 8.6
You will know there is none like our God...

Shemot 8.18

וְהִפְלֵיתִי בַיּוֹם הַהוּא אֶת־אֶרֶץ גֹּשֶׁן אֲשֶׁר עַמִּי עֹמֵד עָלֶיהָ לְבִלְתִּי הֱיוֹת־שָׁם עָרֹב לְמַעַן תֵּדַע כִּי אֲנִי יְהוָֹה בְּקֶרֶב הָאָרֶץ:

Exodus 8.18
You will know that I am The Lord in the midst of the earth...

Shemot 9.29

וַיֹּאמֶר אֵלָיו מֹשֶׁה כְּצֵאתִי אֶת־הָעִיר אֶפְרֹשׂ אֶת־כַּפַּי אֶל־יְהֹוָה הַקֹּלוֹת יֶחְדָּלוּן וְהַבָּרָד לֹא יִהְיֶה־עוֹד לְמַעַן תֵּדַע כִּי לַיהֹוָה הָאָרֶץ:

Exodus 9.29
You will know that the earth belongs to The Lord...

Each of these verses have a Word in common, תֵּדַע Tay Dah, meaning 'to know'. The Gematria is 474. Dear Ones, there are many places in Ha Torah where the Letter ת Tav is added to the front of a Word. I am going to share several examples about the placement of the Letter ת Tav at the front of a Word. After we review the significance of the place of the Letter Tav we will return to a discussion on the Word תֵּדַע Tay Dah.

For example:
Bereisheit 24.67

וַיְבִאֶהָ יִצְחָק הָאֹהֱלָה שָׂרָה אִמּוֹ וַיִּקַּח אֶת־רִבְקָה **וַתְּהִי־לוֹ** לְאִשָּׁה וַיֶּאֱהָבֶהָ וַיִּנָּחֵם יִצְחָק אַחֲרֵי אִמּוֹ׃ פ

Genesis 24.67

And Isaac brought her to his mother Sarah's tent, and took everything from Aleph to Tav of Rebekah, and Alas she became his wife; and he loved her; and Isaac was comforted after his mother's death.

וַתְּהִי

The ת Tav of the Word Vah Tih Hee meaning, and alas... lo... or behold... is not part of the normal Word.. הי The Letter in front of the ת Tav is a ו Vav. The Letter Vav is a connecting Letter. It is not part of the Word either. What we are observing here is reasonably common. Yet, this is <u>very</u> significant. Whenever the Letter ת Tav precedes the beginning of a Word that it normally is not a part of this is an אות Oht, 'sign' for the Torah student to dig around some, mine here, explore here…

Keep in mind that Rivkah was only three years of age and that it would be another nine years before their marriage would be consummated physically. So why was the Word הִי changed to וַתְּהִי ? One may not know why. It may not be revealed to us in this year's Torah Cycle. Yet one records the question and the Gematria. Each year one continues to return to this question. Through the years the answer becomes apparent. Why was Yitzchok comforted? Our Sages Teach this was followed by three special signs that distinguished Sarah.

First, the Sabbath candles burnt from Erev Sabbath, the evening of the Sabbath until just before the next Erev Sabbath, i.e. for Seven days.

Second, the Challah Bread Sarah made for Avraham and Yitzchok for Sabbath fed the entire community. The Challah multiplied many times over.

Third, the Shechina in the form of a cloud Rested at the entrance of Sarah's Tent. Each of these returned for the entire life of Rivkah. Rabbi Moshe Weissman, The Midrash Says (Brooklyn,

New York: Benei Yakov Publications 1980), pp 227,288

Dear Ones, a great deal of diligent research is necessary to learn Torah Truths and to find answers. The Gematria answer may be in the Word תַּבִּיט Tah Beet meaning to look. Ha Torah Says that Eeris looked back when escaping the cities of doom. Her looking back was a sign. Normally the Word תַּבִּיט is spelled נבט. Notice the Letter נ Nun is removed and the Letter ת Tav is added. Mystically we see two different looks. One look Says to Yitzchok this is the wife for you. He sees the Sabbath candles burnt from Erev Sabbath to the next Erev Sabbath just like they did for his mother, Sarah. He sees the Shechina returned to Rest outside the entrance of Sarah's Tent. He saw the blessing from Rivkah's challah. So Mystically we see many signs.

וַתְּהִי
Vah Tih Hee / and alas, and lo or and behold
ו 6 ת 400 ה 5 י 10 = 421

תַּבִּיט
Tah Beet / to look
ת 400 ב 2 י 10 ט 9 =421

For Example:
Bereisheit 45.27

וַיְדַבְּרוּ אֵלָיו אֵת כָּל־דִּבְרֵי יוֹסֵף אֲשֶׁר דִּבֶּר אֲלֵהֶם וַיַּרְא אֶת־הָעֲגָלוֹת אֲשֶׁר־שָׁלַח יוֹסֵף לָשֵׂאת אֹתוֹ וַתְּחִי רוּחַ יַעֲקֹב אֲבִיהֶם:

And they told him everything from Aleph to Tav of all the Words of Yoseif that were spoken to him and when he saw everything from Aleph to Tav of the wagons to carry him to Yoseif, the Spirit of Yaakov their father, revived. This Gematria is a another special Mystical Sign. Yaakov mourns for the loss of his son Yoseif for 22 years. Rabbi Moshe Weissman, The Midrash Says (Brooklyn, New York: Benei Yakov Publications 1980), p 358.

Yaakov searches his life to find what sin he may have committed to be punished with the loss of his son, Yoseif. Why? Just as Yoseif was stripped of his colorful prayer garment Yaakov felt stripped of the blessing of being the chosen of The Lord God. Yaakov knew that the existence of the universes depended upon twelve sons, i.e. twelve tribes were required because there twelve zodiacs. He felt like a reproach! He felt like the merit of being selected to establish the twelve tribes was stripped away from him because of his sin. So Mystically we see the Gematria of וַתְּחִי Vah Tih Chee meaning living, life and the Word חַטָאתוֹ sin share the same Gematrias Chah Taw Toh. Yaakov was concerned that his sin prevented him from establishing the twelve tribes.

וַתְּחִי
Vah Tih Chee / living, life and the Word
424 = 10 י 8 ח 400 ת 6 ו

חַטָאתוֹ
Chah Taw Toh / sin
424 = ת6 ו 400 ת 1 א 9 ט 8 ח

The Letter ת Tav reminds us that this is a sign. We need to check out the sign here. We need to mine here. We need to discover what the intended meaning is. The not so clear meaning is what we need to discover. Why was the Letter ה removed from חיה meaning living thing, Spirit, Life and why was the Letter Tav ת added? There are a number of courses we could take. We could compare the Gematria of 23 for חיה and the Gematria for 424 ותחי. If we subtract 23 from 424 we get 401 which is the difference between the two. There are many possibilities. Each is valuable. We must determine which fits the text. The point is that the normal Gematria for the word חיה has been altered to וַתְּחִי - there is an important reason. To find the answer we mine and research and study to learn why.

Dear Ones, we are now returning to a discussion on the Word תֵּדַע Tay Dah, meaning to know. As pointed out above there were four areas The Lord God Wanted Pharaoh to know. If the emphasis were just on knowing the Word that was used would most likely have been יֵדַע Yoh Day Ah meaning 'To know', however, the Letter י Yud was removed and replaced with the Letter ת Tav. This is unique because the Letter י Yud is the smallest of all Hebrew Letters. The י Yud is also the Letter which represents power. The Yud is replaced with the Letter Tav which Represents Truth and Mystical Signs. ת Tav is the last Letter of the א Aleph ב Bet on Earth but the First Letter of the א Aleph ב Bet in Heaven. So we Observe the Creator Chose Letters that were less threatening. Our Creator did not use the Powerful Letters when expressing what He Wanted Pharaoh to know. Instead the Creator Chose the Letter ת Tav which represents Signs and Truth. Pharaoh would see the great Power of the Creator. It seems Pharaoh's issues would be with understanding the Signs and knowing / Learning the Truth. This Teaches us that there times when Words of Truth must replace Words of Power. I added Learning. Lets return to the four Verses we began with.

Exodus 7.17
'...You will know that I am The Lord...'

'...You will **learn** that I am The Lord...'

Exodus 8.6
You will know there is none like our God...

You will **learn** there is none like our God...

Exodus 8.18
You will know that I am The Lord in the midst of the earth...

You will **learn** that I am The Lord in the midst of the earth...

Exodus 9.29
You will know that the earth belongs to The Lord...

You will **learn** that the earth belongs to The Lord...

What we have just done is to place the emphasis on learning so that one may know. Is it possible our Creator was Teaching Pharaoh a lesson or two? The Gematria for the Word תִלְמַד Tee Lih Mahd meaning to Learn is 474. We, the Jewish People, find the Word תִלְמַד Tee Lih Mahd twice in Ha Torah.

Devarim 14.23

וְאָכַלְתָּ לִפְנֵי ׀ יְהוָה אֱלֹהֶיךָ בַּמָּקוֹם אֲשֶׁר־יִבְחַר לְשַׁכֵּן

שִׂמוֹ שָׁם מַעְשַׂר דְּגָנְךָ תִּירֹשְׁךָ וְיִצְהָרֶךָ וּבְכֹרֹת בְּקָרְךָ
וְצֹאנֶךָ לְמַעַן **תִּלְמַד** לְיִרְאָה אֶת־יְהֹוָה אֱלֹהֶיךָ כָּל־הַיָּמִים:

Deuteronomy 14.23

*And you shall eat before The Lord your God, in the place which He Shall Choose to place His Name there, the tithe of your grain, of your wine, and of your oil, and the firstlings of your herds and of your flocks; that you may **learn** to fear The Lord your God always.*

Devarim 18.9

כִּי אַתָּה בָּא אֶל־הָאָרֶץ אֲשֶׁר־יְהֹוָה אֱלֹהֶיךָ נֹתֵן לָךְ לֹא־
תִלְמַד לַעֲשׂוֹת כְּתוֹעֲבֹת הַגּוֹיִם הָהֵם:

Deuteronomy 18.9

*When you come into the land which The Lord your God Gives you, you shall not **learn** to do after the abominations of those nations.*

We see the relationship between these Verses and the Gematria of 474.

תֵּדַע
Tay Dah, / to know
474 = 70 ע 4 ד 400 ת

תִּלְמַד
Tee Lih Mahd / to Learn
474 = 4 ד 30 מ 30 ל 400 ת

Shoresh, the Hebrew root for תִּלְמַד is לָמַד
Law Mahd [Limood]. At B'nai Noach Torah Institute, LLC we Teach Limood to Noachides / Non-Jews. In our discussion, the Letter ת Tav is added to the beginning of the Word. The Gematria is altered. Mystically we Observe that Our Creator is Teaching Pharaoh. We also learn that we are not to learn, i.e. study etc. abominations of other nations or our own. This means that individuals like myself should not Teach the People of Israel about the abominations of the religions of the world. We, the Jewish People, are to learn Ha Torah. We may Teach as our Creator did with Pharaoh.

Exodus 7.17
*'...You will **learn** that I am The Lord...'*

Exodus 8.6
*'You will **learn** there is none like our God...'*

Exodus 8.18
*'You will **learn** that I am The Lord in the midst of the earth...'*

Exodus 9.29
*'You will **learn** that the earth belongs to The Lord...'*

We need to know through learning. Our Creator Said Avraham, Yitzchok and Yaakov only knew Him as Almighty Shaddai. What do we know Him As? How do we know our Creator?

Exodus 6.7
'...You will know [וִידַעְתֶּם] *that The Lord is your / our God...'*

The acts [of destruction were] acts of great Judgment... This was originally a helpless poor nation. The nation of Egypt was powerful and greatly feared!

Exodus 7.5
Egypt will then know [וְיָדְעוּ] that I am The Lord when I send forth My Hand over Egypt.'

Exodus 9.16
Never the Less, for this reason I have let you survive to show you My Strength so that My Name will be declared throughout the earth.

Pharaoh was a man that needed to be broken so he could learn. Egypt was a powerful country that injured and murdered The People of Israel. The Lord God Dealt with them. He broke them and punished them so that they might realize Truth and reverse their improper acts. The Lord God Drove the message home... the lessons home to Pharaoh and to the people of Egypt. **There are those that must learn from their own mistakes and there are those that can learn from the mistakes of others.**

If we fail to tell the story about how The Lord God Made a mockery of the people of Egypt and of the Great Miracles He Performed in

Delivering the People of Israel, then the People of Israel will not know the Lord. Our sons will not know! Our daughters will not know! Jews who have drifted away from Torah Observances will not know. WE MUST DRAMATICLY TELL THIS STORY!! The story of our deliverance is powerful.

Parshat Shemot Va'eira

Exodus 10.1 - 13.16

What Do We Learn From Three Days?

Shemot 10.21

וַיֹּאמֶר יְהֹוָה אֶל־מֹשֶׁה נְטֵה יָדְךָ עַל־הַשָּׁמַיִם וִיהִי חֹשֶׁךְ עַל־אֶרֶץ מִצְרָיִם וְיָמֵשׁ חֹשֶׁךְ:

Exodus 10.21

And He, The Lord Said to Moshe stretch out your hand towards the Heavens, And it happened Darkness came upon the land of Mitzrayim **and the darkness was felt.**

Our Sages Teach The Lord God Sent darkness and it was dark. They explain the meaning with a story. There was a master whose slave sinned against him, the Master commanded that the slave be given fifty lashes. However, the man who administered the lashes gave a hundred lashes, adding fifty of his own. This is what happened. The Holy One send darkness upon the land of Egypt; but the darkness added feeling. It is like the darkness adding magnitude to the darkness. It is like the darkness doubled the ferocity of the darkness. This is the meaning of the Torah Words, 'darkness was felt'. The darkness had substance.

Dear Ones, we Observe a uniqueness that is rare in Ha Torah, i.e. the repetition of three Letters of Ha Torah in just two Words. Notice שְׁלֹשֶׁת יָמִים Sh Loh Sheht - Yaw Meem, meaning three days. Notice every other Letter repeats. We have שׁ Shin ל Lamid שׁ Shin ת Tav, י Yud מ Mem י Yud ם Mem. This has special significance. We observe three Letters repeated twice in two Words. We have three sets. What does this mean? What do we Observe?

שְׁלֹשֶׁת יָמִים

Beginning on the right going left we have שׁ Shin ל Lamid שׁ Shin ת Tav, followed by י Yud מ Mem י Yud ם Mem. There are two sets of three Letters.

The Letter י Yud represents strength. The second י Yud intensifies the strength of the first ׳ Yud.

What is the meaning of THICK DARKNESS? R. Abdimi of Haifa Said: 'The darkness was doubled and redoubled.' Shemo'R 14.3   We Mystically see what the Rabbi meant when we see with the two Letters of Yud.

Shemot 10.22

וַיֵּט מֹשֶׁה אֶת־יָדוֹ עַל־הַשָּׁמָיִם וַיְהִי חֹשֶׁךְ־אֲפֵלָה בְּכָל־אֶרֶץ מִצְרַיִם **שְׁלֹשֶׁת יָמִים**:

Exodus 10.22

And Moshe stretched forth everything from the Letter Aleph to the Letter Tav of his hand up towards the Heavens and it happened, a thick heavy darkness came upon all the land of Mitzrayim **for three days**.

Where did the darkness come from? R. Judah said: From the darkness above, for it says: He made darkness His hiding place, His pavilion round about Him. Psalms 18.12, R. Nehemiah

Said: It came from the darkness of Gehinnom, for it says: A land of thick darkness, as darkness itself; a land of the shadow of death, without any order. Job 10. 22.

Again we see double Letters. The darkness is represented by the Letters Shin came from the Heaven and from beneath the earth. Darkness is represented by the double Letters of the Shin. The center Letter for חֹשֶׁךְ Cho Sheck, meaning darkness is the Letter שׁ Shin.

There was a thick heavy darkness that could be felt upon the heavens as described in Verse 10.21, i.e. עַל־הַשָּׁמַיִם on the Heavens.

Shemot 10.21

וַיֹּאמֶר יְהוָה אֶל־מֹשֶׁה נְטֵה יָדְךָ עַל־הַשָּׁמַיִם וִיהִי חֹשֶׁךְ עַל־אֶרֶץ מִצְרָיִם וְיָמֵשׁ חֹשֶׁךְ׃

Exodus 10.21

And the Lord said to Moses, Stretch out your hand **toward The Heavens,** *that there may be darkness over the land of Egypt, darkness which may be felt.*

Then there was a thick heavy darkness that could be felt covering the earth as described in Verse 10.22.

Shemot 10.22

וַיֵּט מֹשֶׁה אֶת־יָדוֹ עַל־הַשָּׁמָיִם וַיְהִי חֹשֶׁךְ־אֲפֵלָה בְּכָל־אֶרֶץ מִצְרַיִם שְׁלֹשֶׁת יָמִים:

Exodus 10.22

And Moses stretched out his hand toward heaven; **and there was a thick darkness in all the land of Egypt** *three days;*

Now we know that there is no Letter Shin in the Word אֶרֶץ land or אֲדָמָה earth. However, we do know that the earth is a 360 degree circle so to speak. The second Shin represents the earth in this way. The Gematria for the spelling of the Letter Shin is 360, .

שִׁין
Shin / 360 circle
360 = 50 ן –1 י 300 ש

The last set of Letters are the Letters Mem. They represent the two times the Word Mitzrayim was used in connection with heavy thick darkness in the Heavens and with heavy thick darkness in the earth. Notice the Hebrew Words for מִצְרַיִם Egypt and for חֹשֶׁךְ that follow.

Shemot 10.21, 22
מִצְרַיִם (Mitzrayim / Egypt)

וַיֹּאמֶר יְהֹוָה אֶל־מֹשֶׁה נְטֵה יָדְךָ עַל־הַשָּׁמַיִם וִיהִי חֹשֶׁךְ עַל־אֶרֶץ **מִצְרָיִם** וְיָמֵשׁ חֹשֶׁךְ: וַיֵּט מֹשֶׁה אֶת־יָדוֹ עַל־הַשָּׁמָיִם וַיְהִי חֹשֶׁךְ־אֲפֵלָה בְּכָל־אֶרֶץ **מִצְרַיִם** שְׁלֹשֶׁת יָמִים: לֹא־רָאוּ אִישׁ אֶת־אָחִיו וְלֹא־קָמוּ אִישׁ מִתַּחְתָּיו שְׁלֹשֶׁת יָמִים וּלְכָל־בְּנֵי יִשְׂרָאֵל הָיָה אוֹר בְּמוֹשְׁבֹתָם:

Shemot 10.21, 22
חֹשֶׁךְ (Darkness)

וַיֹּאמֶר יְהֹוָה אֶל־מֹשֶׁה נְטֵה יָדְךָ עַל־הַשָּׁמַיִם וִיהִי **חֹשֶׁךְ** עַל־אֶרֶץ מִצְרָיִם וְיָמֵשׁ **חֹשֶׁךְ**: וַיֵּט מֹשֶׁה אֶת־יָדוֹ עַל־הַשָּׁמָיִם וַיְהִי **חֹשֶׁךְ**־אֲפֵלָה בְּכָל־אֶרֶץ מִצְרַיִם שְׁלֹשֶׁת יָמִים: לֹא־רָאוּ אִישׁ אֶת־אָחִיו וְלֹא־קָמוּ אִישׁ מִתַּחְתָּיו שְׁלֹשֶׁת יָמִים וּלְכָל־בְּנֵי יִשְׂרָאֵל הָיָה אוֹר בְּמוֹשְׁבֹתָם:

Our Rabbis Teach that there were three periods of darkness. These periods of darkness are Mystically represented by the Words חֹשֶׁךְ Darkness.

There were seven days of darkness. During the first three days, one who was sitting and wished to stand could do so, and the one who stood could sit down if he wished. Concerning these days Ha Torah Says,

Darkness 1
And there was a thick heavy darkness in all the Land of Egypt three days; and they could not see one an other... Exodus 10.22, 23

Darkness 2
During the last three days, he who sat could not stand up, he who stood could not sit down, and he who was lying down could not raise himself upright; and concerning these days it says:

Nor could anyone rise from his place for three days... Exodus 10.23

It was during the three days of thick darkness that our Creator, Gave special favor to the People of Israel in the eyes of the Egyptians, so that they lent them everything. The People of Israel would enter the house of the residences of

Mitzrayim to search for gold and silver vessels, and clothing etc. They would request these items from the people of Mitzrayim and they would respond, 'We have nothing to lend you.' however, The People of Israel would find the items and The Egyptians would reason to themselves: 'They could have taken these items without asking but instead asked for them. So they lent the items of gold, silver etc to The People of Israel. This was in fulfillment to the prophecy to Avram in Genesis 15.14. *'Afterward shall they come out with great substance...'* How was this possible? Genesis 10.3 say, '...all the People of Israel had light in their dwellings...' but Scripture does not say in the land of Goshen. Why? Our Sages Say, to show that wherever a Jew went, light accompanied him and illumined what was within the barrels, boxes, and treasure-chests. What was the Light that lit their way? This was the revelation of God's Word. Our Sages Teach - *Your word is a lamp unto my feet and a light to my pathway...* Psalms 119.105

These were the double three days of darkness,i.e. six days of darkness.

Third Darkness

The Seventh Day

The seventh day of darkness was a day of darkness at the sea of Reeds, as it says: *'There was the cloud that came between them [the people of Mitzrayim and The People of Israel] and the cloud gave darkness for the people of Mitzrayim and the pillar of fire gave light at night for The People of Israel...* Exodus 14.19,20

As a result we say, *The Lord is my light and my salvation* Ps. XXVII. In the Messianic Age The Lord God will bring darkness [to sinners, but light to Israel,] as it says,

Isaiah 60.2-5

Arise, shine; for your light has come, and the glory of the Lord has risen upon you. For, behold, the darkness shall cover the earth, and thick darkness the people; but the Lord shall arise upon you, and his glory shall be seen upon you. And the nations shall come to your light, and kings to the brightness of your rising. Lift up your eyes around, and see; all they gather themselves together, they come to you; your sons shall come from far, and your daughters shall be nursed at your side. Then you shall see, and be filled with light, and your heart shall fear, and be enlarged; because the abundance of the sea shall be turned to you, the wealth of the nations shall come to you.

Parshat Shemot Beshalach

Exodus 13.17 - 17.16

Can One Be Thankful Enough?

The Gematria of 100
In the Book of Shemot / Exodus The Word הָעָם Haw Awm meaning 'The People' or the Nation occurs 100 times. To me this is like the Creator of the Universe Speaking to our father Avraham in Genesis 12 Saying לֶךְ־לְךָ. Remember the chapter's discussion where we discussed unique Words in Ha Torah? We discussed unique rotations of Letters. Remember how every other Letter followed? We have the same uniqueness in לֶךְ־לְךָ meaning, 'Go' 'Get out!' The Gematria of לֶךְ־לְךָ. is 100. So here, in the Book of Shemot it is like 'The Nation' 'The Holy Nation' 'The People of Israel' see the gates of freedom being opened and the Creator of the universe Saying to the People 'Go' 'Get Out' of Mitzrayim, leave slavery

behind. Flee to freedom!! The Word עַל meaning to rise up or be upon also has the Gematria of 100. Mystically it is like the People of Israel rise up.

לֶךְ־לְךָ
Lech Lecha / 'Go' 'Get out!'
100 = 20 ךְ 30 ל   20 ךָ 30 ל

עַל
Ahl / Rise Upon
100 = 30 ל 70 ע

In Parshat Beshalach הָעָם occurs 18 times. The חַי meaning life is the Gematria 18. Mystically Egypt gave birth and Yisroel was given life.

חַי
Chai / Life
18 = 10 י 8 ח

In this week's Parshat the Word הָעָם takes on very significance meaning.

Shemot 13.17, 18

וַיְהִי בְּשַׁלַּח פַּרְעֹה **אֶת־הָעָם** וְלֹא־נָחָם אֱלֹהִים דֶּרֶךְ אֶרֶץ פְּלִשְׁתִּים כִּי קָרוֹב הוּא כִּי ׀ אָמַר אֱלֹהִים פֶּן־יִנָּחֵם **הָעָם** בִּרְאֹתָם מִלְחָמָה וְשָׁבוּ מִצְרָיְמָה: וַיַּסֵּב אֱלֹהִים ׀ **אֶת־הָעָם** דֶּרֶךְ הַמִּדְבָּר יַם־סוּף וַחֲמֻשִׁים עָלוּ בְנֵי־יִשְׂרָאֵל מֵאֶרֶץ מִצְרָיִם:

Exodus 13.17, 18

And it came happened, when Pharaoh had let **everything from the Letter Aleph to the Letter Tav of the people go,** *that God led them not through the way of the land of the Philistines, although that was near; for God Said, Lest perhaps* **the people** *change their minds when they see war, and they return to Mitzrayim. Instead, God Led* **everything from the Letter Aleph to the Letter Tav of the people** *around, through the way of the wilderness of the Red Sea; and B'nei Yisrael went up armed out of the land of Mitzrayim.*

Note the Word הָעָם occurs three times. We are going to Mystically examine what each Letter may represent.

The Letter ה Hey = 5 is Represented by חמש
5 Books of Moses Chumash = 5
1/5 of Yisrael came out of Mitzrayim
Yisroel came out of Mitzrayim armed
Rabbi Avrohom Davis, The Mesudah Chumash A New Linear Translation Exodus (Hoboken New Jersey, KTVA Publishing House, Inc., 1993) pp 156, 157

3 x 5 = 15

The Letter ע Ayin = 70 represents:
Yoseif's 70 languages - Rabbi Moshe Weissman, The Midrash Says (Brooklyn, New York: Benei Yakov Publications 1980), p. 390
Yaakov's 70 descendants who went down to Mitzrayim - Genesis 46.27, Exodus 1.5
Yisroel's 70 Elders - Exodus 24.1

3 x 70 = 210

The Letter מ Mem = 40 represents:
Moshe in Mitzrayim 40 years
Moshe in Midian 40 years

Moshe in Midbar / the Wilderness 40 years
Rabbi Yisrael Yitzchok Yishai Chasidah, Encyclopedia of Biblical Personalities (Jerusalem: Shaar Press Publication Mashabim, 2003) p340 Midrash Bereisheit Rabba 100.10

3 x 40 = 120

345 = 15 + 210 + 120

מֹשֶׁה

Moses

345 = 5 ה 300 ש 40 מ

הָעָם / Haw Awm
The People
115 = 40 ם 70 ע 5 ה

עֲלִיָה
Ah Lee Yawh
Arise Ascend up

115 = 5 ה 10 י 30 ל 70 ע

We are the people who were delivered from

Mitzrayim by The Lord God to arise to go up.

חָזָק

Ha Zak Strong

115 = 100 ק 7 ז 8 ח

We are the people who must be strong in learning and Observing HaTorah.

Dear Ones, we were standing at the red sea. Pharaoh and his elite army were charging toward us. We were frightened beyond measure. The אֶת־הָעָם eht of Haw Awm / The People, included all our emotions. We had plenty of emotions. This was an emotional time for us. Some of us were angry. Within us as fear, anger, complaints and wild imaginations of what might happen. Yet, by the powerful hand of The Lord God we were delivered and our enemy defeated! Blessed be The Name of The Lord God who Delivered us!! After our deliverance an emotion deep within the heart of every Jew and convert who were delivered that day was a song. The song of Shemot 15 sprung out of us. The song in us is part of the Aleph Tav, i.e the Eth everything from the first Letter of the Aleph Bet, i.e 'The Aleph' to the Last Letter, i.e. 'The Tav'. The Gematria for this song is 516. The Gematria for Eht Haw Am the people is also 516.

אֶת־הָעָם
Eht Haw Am the people
א 1 ת 400   ה 5 ע 70 ם 40 = 516

אָשִׁירָה
Aw Shee Raw / to Sing
א 1 שׁ 300 י 10 ר 200 ה 5 = 516

שִׁירוּ
Shee Ru / Sing
שׁ 300 י 10 ר 200 וּ 6 = 516

Shemot 15.1

אָז יָשִׁיר־מֹשֶׁה וּבְנֵי יִשְׂרָאֵל אֶת־הַשִּׁירָה הַזֹּאת לַיהוָה וַיֹּאמְרוּ לֵאמֹר **אָשִׁירָה** לַיהוָה כִּי־גָאֹה גָּאָה סוּס וְרֹכְבוֹ רָמָה בַיָּם׃

Exodus 15.1
Then sang Moses and the people of Israel

*this song to the Lord, and spoke, saying, I will **sing** to the Lord, for he has triumphed gloriously; the horse and his rider has he thrown into the sea.*

Shemot 15.21

וַתַּעַן לָהֶם מִרְיָם **שִׁירוּ** לַיהוָה כִּי־גָאֹה גָּאָה סוּס וְרֹכְבוֹ רָמָה בַיָּם:

Exodus 15.21

*And Miriam answered them, **Sing** to the Lord, for he has triumphed gloriously; the horse and his rider has he thrown into the sea.*

Dear Ones, many of you have shown respect and appreciation to me. Thank you! This type of appreciation is what we need to show to our Creator, The Lord God. We should be thankful for every breath for everything our Creator Gives us each day. Revi and I try to teach our children to be appreciative. Saying thank you shows appreciation. Children who do not show appreciation to their parents cannot show appreciation to The Lord God. One cannot say, I love The Lord but hate my parents who brought me into this world. It is The Lord who Teaches children to love and to honor their parents. What is a child going to say to the Lord? I love you but I don't like the Commandment to love and honor my parents. Love is NOT just a word. (Love is seen by the actions it prompts) Love is the action behind the Word. Can we see how we cannot say we Love The Lord yet openly and defyingly violate His Commands. A child who does not communicate i.e write, text message, e-mail, phone or visit her / his parents cannot love the Lord! IT IS IMPOSSIBLE!! So we must try to keep the Observances of Ha Torah. Appreciation is a very important. We see this appreciation in the full hearted emotions and in the enthusiasm of those who sang with all they had to The Lord for delivering them and defeating their enemy.

Dear Friends, we the Jewish people are more than 3,326 years from the day when our Creator delivered our parents from Mitzrayim. Still we continue to say thank you our Lord God for delivering us from Mitzrayim and from slavery everyday. We have been saying thank you for over 3,000 years. What is the point? Think about this, Saying thank you each day for a year is like saying thank you a thousand time and THAT says something about being thankful!

Can one be thank enough?

Parshat Shemot Yitro

Exodus 18.1 - 20.23

What is Prophecy?

Dear Friends, there are two Words in this Passuk that really reach out and grab my attention.

Shemot 18.21

וְאַתָּה **תֶחֱזֶה** מִכָּל־הָעָם אַנְשֵׁי־**חַיִל** יִרְאֵי אֱלֹהִים אַנְשֵׁי אֱמֶת שֹׂנְאֵי בָצַע וְשַׂמְתָּ עֲלֵהֶם שָׂרֵי אֲלָפִים שָׂרֵי מֵאוֹת שָׂרֵי חֲמִשִּׁים וְשָׂרֵי עֲשָׂרֹת: כב

Exodus 18.21

And you shall **prophetically choose** *from all the people* **capable** *men, who fear God, men of truth, hating unjust gain; and place such over them, to be leaders of thousands, and leaders of hundreds, leaders of fifties, and leaders of tens...*

תֶּחֱזֶה

Teh Chaw Zeh / Prophetically choose
What does it mean to prophetically choose?
If an individual is prophetic as Moshe was they have a history of and an ability of being able to see the future close up and at a distance.

Shemot 2.11,12

וַיְהִי ׀ בַּיָּמִים הָהֵם וַיִּגְדַּל מֹשֶׁה וַיֵּצֵא אֶל־אֶחָיו **וַיַּרְא** בְּסִבְלֹתָם **וַיַּרְא** אִישׁ מִצְרִי מַכֶּה אִישׁ־עִבְרִי מֵאֶחָיו:

וַיִּפֶן כֹּה וָכֹה **וַיַּרְא** כִּי אֵין אִישׁ וַיַּךְ אֶת־הַמִּצְרִי וַיִּטְמְנֵהוּ בַּחוֹל:

Exodus 2.11,12

And it happened in those days, when Moses was grown, that he went out to his brothers, and **[prophetically]** *looked through their compulsory service; that* **he saw** *an Egyptian beating a Hebrew, one of his brothers. And* **he [prophetically] looked** *this way and that way, and when* **he saw** *that there was no man, he slew the Egyptian, and hid him in the sand.*

Our Sages speak of Moshe's prophetic ability in Exodus 2.12 and in Shemot Rabah 1.28,29.

בְּסִבְלֹתָם

Moshe prophetically reviewed their compulsory service - What did he see?

The Rabbis said: The taskmasters were Egyptians taskmasters who were over ten Jewish officers. The Jewish officer was over ten Israelites. The taskmasters used to go to the Jewish Officers' houses early in the morning, at cock-crow to drag them out to work.

Moshe saw that an Egyptian taskmaster went to the home of a Jewish Officer. He set eyes on the Jewish Officer's wife. She was beautiful without blemish. He made a plan to take her. He waited for the cock-crow. He forced the Jewish Officer to go to work. Then returned to this Jewish Officer's house and lay down with the woman who thought that it was her husband. She became pregnant from him. When her husband returned, he discovered the Egyptian taskmaster emerging from his house. The Husband asked wife, 'Did he touch you?'

His wife replied: 'Yes, I thought it was you.'

Later, the Egyptian taskmaster realized that he was caught. He made the Jewish Officer return to his hard labor, smiting him and trying to slay him. Moshe saw this. He prophetically knew by means of the Holy Spirit what had happened in the Jewish man's house. He knew the Egyptian taskmaster was going to kill the Jewish Officer.

What did Moshe do? He reasoned. He appealed to the heavenly court. The Angels quoted twice from Ha Torah,

Shemot 21.12 -
He who strikes a man, so that he dies, shall be surely put to death.

Vayikra 20.10
And the man who commits adultery with another man's wife, he who commits adultery with his neighbor's wife, the adulterer and the adulteress shall surely be

put to death.

So Ha Torah Says, Moshe *[prophetically] looked this way and that way,* meaning, Moshe viewed the Egyptian Taskmasters past, present and future and found him entirely void. No good would come from this man. Our Sages said: Moshe saw that there was no hope that righteous persons would arise from him or his offspring until the end of generations. There was no man to say a good word in his behalf. Moshe said to the Heavenly court, 'This man deserves death.' They agreed. The Heavenly court found him guilty of the charges of theft, rape, adultery and intent to murder. Sentence was passed. He is to die.

Moshe thought, 'Who is to be zealous for God and slay him?' So Moshe smote the Egyptian taskmaster. The Rabbis Say that Moshe pronounced God's Name against him and thus slew him.

We also see this Prophetical Vision with Avraham in Genesis 18.1 when Ha Torah Says *'Hashem*

Appeared to Avram in the groves of Mamrei...' So we have a basis for the Word וַיֵּרָא meaning to see prophetically. So we see the foundation in Ha Torah and the Midrash for Prophetic Vision and how Prophetic Vision operates even though the nekudot / vowels are different.

Yitro's criteria is:
Yitro, a Noachide, a Jewish Convert and the Father - in - Law of Moshe realizes that Moshe has this very unique Prophetic gift from God and he Instructs Moshe to Prophetically choose men with three qualities. Who has ever heard of prophetically choosing leaders??

Choose *capable men, who fear God*
Many men including myself are not included in this description. When we speak of חַיִל Chah Yeel we are speaking of strong men, efficient men and wealthy men. A wealthy man has resources and assets many of us do not have.

Choose *men who are truthful*
Choose *[men] who hate unjust profit*

Mystically the Word חַיִל Chah Yeel / capable moves in a progression from right to left, 48 ◄ = 30 ל + ◄ = 10 י + ◄ = 8 ח.

When we study the Gematria 48 we return to the very first time in Ha Torah where the Gematria 48 occurs, Genesis 3.14 with the Word, חַיֶּיךָ Chah Yaw Chaw, meaning life, live. חי Chai has one י Yud. חַיֶּיךָ has two. There are a number of possibilities for this. The Letter י Yud represents strength. Here we observe double the strength in the Word חַיֶּיךָ life. One could say a Yud is for this life and a Yud is for the next life. Notice the progression, 48 + 20 + 10 + 10 + 8.

חַיִל
Chah Yeel / Capable
48 = 30 ל 10 י 8 ח

חַיֶּיךָ
Chah Yaw Chaw / Life, Live
48 = 20 ך 10 י 10 י 8 ח

In Genesis 3.14 the Creator Passed Judgment on the serpent. The serpent would crawl on his belly all the days of his חַיֶּיךָ life, with an emphasis of, life / live, being very long. Yet the progression of the Letters indicate unity. So the serpent would crawl on his belly all the days of his life. Yet the end result would be life. The plan for the serpent was life. The Word חַיֶּיךָ shows us this plan. The serpent is returning. The serpent is going in the same direction. From this we learn of the importance of following the Path of Ha Torah which also goes in one direction. When we consider the Word חַיִל Chah Yeel / capable we again observe one direction. Mystically we see stability. We see a planned course. The capable man is ALWAYS TRUTHFUL! - Truthfulness is one direction. The capable man ALWAYS HATES UNJUST PROFITS. Again, a capable man is traveling in one direction, which is the direction of honesty, purity, righteousness.

Let's discuss תֶּחֱזֶה Teh Chaw Zeh / Prophetically choose... The Gematria is 420. The direction is different. Prophecy flows from our Creator Who is Represented by the Letter ת Tav in Earth and the Letter א Aleph in The Heavens. This is a principle of Gematria that is called At Bash.

Things in the Heavens are reversed from things on earth.

B'nai Noach Torah Institute, LLC provides a FREE COPY of the At Bash Chart to ANYONE who requests one. Simply ask for the At Bash Chart.

Knowledge, i.e. prophecy flows from the Creator to the Novie, the Prophet who only sees prophecy with limited vision. This is represented by the numbers and Letters of תֶחֱזֶה Teh Chaw Zeh.

420 ◀ = 5 ה + ◀ = 7 ז + ◀ = 8 ח + ◀ = 400 ת.

The first occurrence of the Gematria 420 is in Genesis 1.2 where Mystically we Observe that the World הָיְתָה 'BECAME' void and desolate then The Breath of God moved upon the surface of the water and God Said 'Let My Light be revealed.'

When a world is in chaos and the Spirit of the Creator Moves upon it, change is going to happen. When The Lord God Reveals His Light, i.e. Ha Torah, the world of chaos takes on structure.

What does *Became void and desolate* make reference to? There are many possibilities. Our Sages refer to the first 2,000 years From Creation as Void. Why? The beings in the World were destroyed in the Noach Flood in 1656 From Creation because they became void and desolate. Ha Torah was not observed. *The world is to exist six thousand years. In the first two thousand there was desolation; followed by two thousand years the Torah flourished which is followed by two thousand years of the Messianic era...'* Sanhedrin 97a

Our Creator Formed us וַיִּיצֶר with two strong personalities. The Yeter Tov and Yetzer Raw. Rabbi Meir Zlotowitz and Rabbi Nosson Scherman, The Artscroll Tanach Series - Bereishis Vol. I(a) (Brooklyn, New York: Mesorah Publications, Ltd. 3rd Impression, 1989), p 189, Rabbi Moshe Weissman, The Midrash Says (Brooklyn, New York: Benei Yakov Publications

Our Creator gave Adam and Chavah Seven Laws, the Sages Teach, Six at Creation and one later. Genesis 2.16 Yet, the beings on earth would not follow the Observances.

The Serpent lusted after Chavah, the wife of Adam. The serpent set a plan in place to separate Chavah from Adam so he could have her sexually. The serpent attempted to take what was NOT his, i.e. steal Chavah from Adam. The serpent attempted to take his neighbor's wife, i.e. adultery. Rabbi Meir Zlotowitz and Rabbi Nosson Scherman, The Artscroll Tanach Series - Bereishis Vol. I(a) (Brooklyn, New York: Mesorah Publications, Ltd. 3rd Impression, 1989), pp 112, 113; Rabbi Moshe Weissman, The Midrash Says (Brooklyn, New York: Benei Yakov Publications 1980), p. 45

Chavah reasoned! She Took! She stole. She gave to her Husband that which she stole. She disobeyed the Command's of Ha Torah. Chavah desired the forbidden fruit from the Tree of

Knowledge of Good and Evil. They repented!

Later Kayin became jealous of his brother Hevel for several reasons. Hevel was born with two twin sisters which became his wives. Kayin was born with one twin sister which became his wife. Kayin was angry that Hevel had two wives. As the older brother he felt like he should have the double blessing, i.e. two wives. Rabbi Avrohom Davis, The Mesudah Chumash A New Linear Translation Bereishis (Hoboken New Jersey, KTVA Publishing House, Inc., 1991) p 42

Kayin was angry with The Lord God so he brought spoiled flax seed as his offering while his brother brought woven wool and goat's hair, the finest cream and cheese from the the very best of his firstborn flocks. Kayin murders his brother. Unfortunately good was taken from the world. Evil remained. Hevel was good. Kayin was evil. What impact did this have? Adam could not marry his daughters, the wives of Hevel. The only mate for Adam was Chavah. At that time the only mate for the two twin daughters was Hevel. Rabbi Moshe Weissman, The Midrash Says

(Brooklyn, New York: Benei Yakov Publications 1980), pp 60 - 62

Adam became angry with Chavah and makes a very poor choice to separate from her. They remained separated for 130 years all the while the evil Kayin populated the world with evil descendants that did not Observe The Torah Given to them by the Creator. Eventually the world was destroyed. This period from creation to after the flood to Avram was known as a period of Void and destruction. Avram lived 52 years in the age of Void and Desolation. Yet at the age of 52 Avram brought Light into the World. We say the World was Created for Ha Torah and Ha Torah for the Jewish People. At the age of 52 years Avram began Teaching Ha Torah. Our Sages Teach that it was then that the Age of Ha Torah began. The Age of Ha Torah is the second period. This would be like Genesis 1.4 where *God Said Let My Light Be Revealed,* i.e. the 613 Observances of Ha Torah be Revealed. Remember the sun and the moon were not Created until day four in Genesis 1.14. So in this sense the World הָיְתָה was void and desolate or the world הָיְתָה became void and desolate. The Gematria of הָיְתָה is 420. We see the relationship between תֶּחֱזֶה Teh Chaw Zehand הָיְתָה Haw Yih Tawh through the Gematria of 420. Mystically we Observe the relationship as a prophecy that took 4,000 years to unfold.

תֶּחֱזֶה
Teh Chaw Zeh / Prophetically [Choose}
420 = 5 ה 7 ז 8 ח 400 ת

הָיְתָה
Haw Yih Tawh / Became... Was
420= 5 ה 400 ת 10 י 5 ה

We are living in the third period. This is the Age of Moshiach / Messiah. The Age of Messiah began 1,774 years ago. We are presently at 5774 From Creation. This age will end in about 226 years. Then the Mystical prophecy of 6,000 years in Genesis 1.1 will be fulfilled. The Letter Aleph = 1,000. 6 x 1,000 = 6,000. The Tanna debe

Eliyahu taught: 'The world is to exist six thousand years; the first two thousand years are to be void; the next two thousand years are the period of the Torah, and the following two thousand years are the period of the Messiah. Rosh Hashana 31a; Sanhedrin 97a; Avoda Zara 9a

Parshat Shemot Mishpatim

Exodus 21.1 - 24.18

Why Do We Observe The Commands Of The Lord God?

Shemot 21.1

וְאֵלֶּה הַמִּשְׁפָּטִים אֲשֶׁר תָּשִׂים לִפְנֵיהֶם

Exodus 21.1
And these are, the Laws that you shall set before them.

What Laws is The Creator Making reference to? The Laws Given on Mt. Sinai and those discussed here.

How are the Laws to be set before them? Like a table is set.

What is the purpose for the Laws?

Observing the Laws brings many Blessings.

וְאֵלֶּה הַמִּשְׁפָּטִים Vih Ay Leh - Ha Meesh Faw Teem, meaning *'And these are The Laws'* is the Gematria 526.

42 = ו6 א1 ל30 ה5
484 = ה5 מ40 ש300 פ80 ט9 י10 ם40
526 = 42 + 484

The people received The Laws from our Creator through the hand of Moshe in 2448 F.C [From Creation]. 430 years earlier in 2030 F. C. [From Creation] our Creator spoke similar Words to our Father Avram.

Bereisheit 15.1
אַחַר ׀ הַדְּבָרִים הָאֵלֶּה הָיָה דְבַר־יְהֹוָה אֶל־אַבְרָם בַּמַּחֲזֶה לֵאמֹר אַל־תִּירָא אַבְרָם אָנֹכִי מָגֵן לָךְ שְׂכָרְךָ הַרְבֵּה מְאֹד:

Genesis 15.1
After these things There Came The Word of The Lord to Abram in a vision, saying, Fear not, Abram; I am your shield, and your reward will be great.

הָיָה דְבַר־יְהֹוָה אֶל־אַבְרָם
There Came The Word of The Lord
to Abram

ה5 י10 ה5 ד4 ב2 ר200 = 226
י10 ה5 ו6 ה5 א1 ל30 = 57
א1 ב2 ר200 ם40 = 243
526 = 226 + 57 = 243

Bereisheit 12.1-3

וַיֹּאמֶר יְהֹוָה אֶל־אַבְרָם לֶךְ־לְךָ מֵאַרְצְךָ וּמִמּוֹלַדְתְּךָ וּמִבֵּית אָבִיךָ אֶל־הָאָרֶץ אֲשֶׁר אַרְאֶךָּ: וְאֶעֶשְׂךָ לְגוֹי גָּדוֹל וַאֲבָרֶכְךָ וַאֲגַדְּלָה שְׁמֶךָ וֶהְיֵה בְּרָכָה: וַאֲבָרְכָה מְבָרְכֶיךָ וּמְקַלֶּלְךָ אָאֹר וְנִבְרְכוּ בְךָ כֹּל מִשְׁפְּחֹת הָאֲדָמָה:

Genesis 12.1-3

And the Lord Had Said to Abram, Get out from your country, and from your family, and from your father's house, to a land that I Will Show you; And I Will Make of you a great nation, and I Will Bless you, and Make your name great; and you shall be a blessing; And I Will Bless those who Bless you, and curse him who curses you; and in you shall all families of the earth be blessed.

וַאֲבָרְכָה מְבָרְכֶיךָ
'And I Will Bless those who Bless you'
234= 5ה 20כ 200ר 2ב 1א 6ו
292 = 20ך 10י 20צ 200ר 2ב 40מ
526 = 234 + 292

Genesis 12.2, 3
'There Came The Word of The Lord to Abram'
'And I Will Bless those who Bless you'
'And these are The Laws'

Mystically we can see the Gematria connection of these three Torah Phrases Each have the Gematria of 526, The Lord God Spoke each. Spiritually we Observe that each require ACTION! Avram Believed! And because Avram Believed the People of Israel could Observe The Laws Given to them. Avram was Blessed. We His descendants can also be blessed like our Father Avraham.

In the final Word מוֹפֵת Moh Fayt meaning, Miracle, Wonder, Marvel, Sign, we Observe the Mystical power through which The Lord God Brings Miracles, Wonders and Blessings to those who Love Him and Observe His Commands.

מוֹפֵת
Moh Fayt / Miracle, Wonder, Marvel, Sign
526 = 400ת 80פ 6ו 40מ

Dear Ones, great blessings result from Obedience to the Laws.

Deuteronomy 7.6-11
For you are a Holy people to The Lord your God; The Lord your God Has Chosen you to be a special people to Himself, above all peoples that are upon the face of the earth. The Lord Did Not set his love upon you, nor Choose you, because you were more in number than any people; for you were the fewest of all peoples; But because the Lord Loved you, and because He Would Keep the oath which He Had sworn to your fathers, The Lord Has Brought you out with a mighty hand, and Redeemed you out of the house of slaves, from the hand of Pharaoh king of Egypt. Know therefore that The Lord your God, He is God, The Faithful God,

Which Keeps Covenant and Mercy with those who love Him and keep His Commandments to a thousand generations; And Repays those who hate Him to their face, to Destroy them; He Will Not be slack to him who hates Him, He Will Repay him to his face. You shall therefore keep The Commandments, and The Statutes, and The Judgments, which I Command you this day, to do them.

Psalms 105.1-10
O give thanks to The Lord; call upon His Name; make known His Deeds among the people. Sing to Him, sing psalms to Him; talk you of all His wondrous works. Glory in His Holy Name; let the heart of those who seek the Lord rejoice. Seek the Lord, and His Strength; seek His Face continually. Remember His Marvelous Works that He Has Done; His Wonders, and the Judgments of His Mouth; O seed of Abraham, His servant! O children of Jacob, His chosen! He is the Lord our God; His judgments are over all the earth. He Has Remembered His covenant for ever, the Word which He Commanded to a thousand

generations. The covenant which He Made with Abraham, and his oath to Isaac; And confirmed the same to Jacob for a Law, and to Israel for an everlasting covenant;

Parshat Shemot Terumah

Exodus 25.1 - 27:19

Why We Should Give?

Shemot 25.1

וַיְדַבֵּר יְהֹוָה אֶל־מֹשֶׁה לֵּאמֹר :

Exodus 25.1
And He, The Lord Spoke to Moshe, Saying,

Shemot 25.2

דַּבֵּר אֶל־בְּנֵי יִשְׂרָאֵל וְיִקְחוּ־לִי תְרוּמָה
מֵאֵת כָּל־אִישׁ אֲשֶׁר יִדְּבֶנּוּ לִבּוֹ תִּקְחוּ
אֶת־תְּרוּמָתִי :

Exodus 25.2
Speak to The People of Israel / the Children of Israel and take a Terumah for Me from every man that is impelled... driven by his heart. Take everything from Aleph to Tav of My Terumah.

אֲשֶׁר יִדְּבֶנּוּ לִבּוֹ
that is impelled... driven by his heart
110 = 6 ו 2 ב 30 ל   6 ו 50 נ 2 ב 4 ד 10 י
501 = 200 ר 300 ש 1 א
611 = 110 + 501

It is from this Parshat of Ha Torah that we learn about the nature of giving... not compelling... not guilt tripping... not motivating... not commanding... just speaking... just taking...

The Word תְּרוּמָה is Torah with the Letter Mem added. When we think of the Torah we think of the giving of Ha Torah on Har Sinai. When we give Terumah the Terumah Offering comes from Ha Torah.

There are many causes to give to. May HaShem Bless our giving.

תּוֹרָה
Torah / Law / Statutes
611 = 5 ה 200 ר 6 ו 400 ת

We already know that one should be driven...

impelled to study, learn and Observe the Torah. Terumah Teaches us that the impelling to give an offering comes from Ha Torah. The Letter Mem is the Gematria 40. When we add the Letter Mem to The Torah we have Terumah. We have the desire to give... the desire to set aside a portion...

The Letter Mem brings acts of kindness, acts of goodness... acts of caring... The Letter Mem is speaking to all the inhabitants of the World. The Letter Mem is Saying that acts of goodness originate in the Torah. The root of goodness is from the Torah. We learn how to care from Ha Torah. The Letter Mem is a continual Letter like a circle. The Letter Mem goes round and round...

Recently, I was sharing about the Mitzvot *Fear Of God*. In this discussion I said we cannot let our hair down, so to speak. Why? We must always be aware of the Presence of our Creator in every action, thought, Word or deed or lack there of. What I did not share is that Fear Of God also includes joyfully giving of money to The Lord God and to others. When an individual gives his valuables to The Lord God it says He is more important. It says, I Love God more than money. Yet, The Lord God ONLY WANTS A PORTION! Our Creator Said to Moshe, 'Speak to The People of Israel.' Speak to the men, women and children. The Lord God Desires that the men give an offering. He Desires that men give a portion of what he, his wife and children have. So He Wants the man to give a portion. He wants the Wife and Children to support his decision and to guide his decision. Give a portion but don't give everything. Then, there are only certain gifts The Lord God Desires.

Shemot 25.3

וְזֹאת הַתְּרוּמָה אֲשֶׁר תִּקְחוּ מֵאִתָּם זָהָב וָכֶסֶף וּנְחֹשֶׁת׃

Exodus 25.3
And this is the offering which you shall take from them; gold, and silver, and bronze:

Dear Ones, within the Word תְּרוּמָה Termuah is the root Word רוּם Room means to elevate to rise to have pride to have haughtiness. Room also means height, elevation. The Terumah Offering is intended to Elevate. It is an offering that one gives upward... that one lifts up to The Lord God. Yet when one does not give the Terumah Offering the opposite happens. They are lifting up them selves.

Parshat Shemot Tezaveh

Exodus 27:20 - 30.10

Why Are The People of Israel Called The Light Of The World?

Shemot 27.20

וְאַתָּה תְּצַוֶּה ׀ אֶת־בְּנֵי יִשְׂרָאֵל וְיִקְחוּ אֵלֶיךָ שֶׁמֶן זַיִת זָךְ כָּתִית לַמָּאוֹר לְהַעֲלֹת נֵר תָּמִיד:

Exodus 27.20
And you shall Command Everything from the Letter Aleph to the Letter Tav of The People of Israel and have them take Pure Olive Oil [which is lightly] crushed to light, to raise the lamp continually.

When I read the Words The Lord God Spoke to Moshe, Mystically several hidden meanings open. The Word תְּצַוֶּה Tih Tzah Veh / Tezaveh is written only one time in Ha Torah where as צִוָּה

Tzee Vawh meaning Command is written 112 times. By definition both Words mean to Command. However when the Letter Tav is added this brings additional Mystical possibilities. Why? This is because the Word Oht The Letter ת Tav was added to the beginning of צִוָּה as a sign for us to closely review this text. There are Mystical Revelations hidden here. The Letter ת Tav is the last Letter of אות Oht meaning SIGN. This is a sign that we are to snoop around, to think over, to mine this text. Immediately the fact that תְּצַוֶּה occurs only one time in all of Ha Torah points to The Lord God Who Is One! The Lord God Is The One Who Gives The Commands. There is only One Command Giver!! In addition when using At Bash The Letter Tav is the First Letter of the Aleph Bet. On earth we begin with the Letter Aleph to ascend to the Heavenly realm. The reverse is true in Heaven. The decent from the Heavens to earth begins with the Letter Tav and ends here on earth with the Letter Aleph. Notice the diagram that follows. In Gematria this is what we refer to as At Bash.

Begin Here from Heaven to Earth

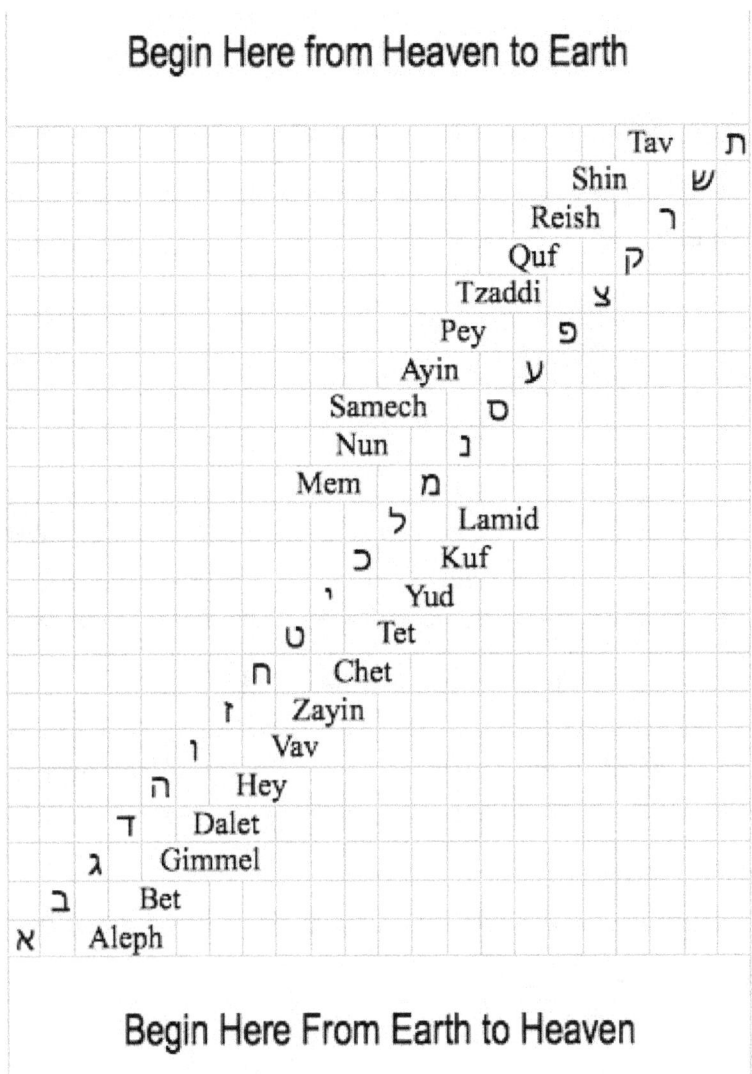

Begin Here From Earth to Heaven

The Gematria of תְּצַוֶּה is 501. This is significant because of the relationship to רֹאשׁ Rosh meaning Head, Front, Top.

תְּצַוֶּה
Tezaveh / And He Commanded
501 = 5 ה 6 ו 90 צ 400 ת

רֹאשׁ
Rosh / Head
501 = 300 שׁ 1 א 200 ר

Now when we return to the Passuk / Verse we focus on the Oil. Why? The Command Given to The People of Israel had to do with the Oil. Rashi Says, This oil was NOT beaten. The finest olives would release oil given slight pressure. This Olive oil is First. This Olive Oil is from the First press. This is the oil used for the Holy Menorah.

Additional oil would be gathered for other purposes. This olive oil is second. The pulp is ground. Oil is extracted. The oil is not clear. The oil is not pure. The oil is clouded with sediment. The Sheh mehn / Oil is like The Lord God Who Is One! The Shemin is Separated from all other Olive Oil for service in the Mishkon. The Shemin is Holy. The Shemin Oil is clear, i.e with out any sediment. The Shemin is Pure.

The olive had to be broken to give forth oil that would be separated for service in the Menorah in the Mishkon. The olive is valuable. Yet the olive must be crushed... pressed until the finest oil came forth. The oil served a vital function in the Mishkon. The oil was the source for giving light in the lamp. We are like this olive. In life there are time we are seriously pressed. These are times we may not understand. Yet the pressing is only for a short time. During these times we give forth oil.

We have a season. Our season may be seventy years or perhaps eighty years... or what our Creator chooses... When our season ends, God Willing, we are ripe with Torah knowledge. And God Willing we give forth the purest clear oil. This means that we have written out thoughts... videoed our understandings to be shared with others, etc.

In this Passuk there is an Observance given to

the Priests that they should always keep the lamp lit and burning. The lamp should not go out. There should always be a supply of oil...

נֵר תָּמִיד
Nahr Taw Meed / Lamp Continually burns
704 = 4ד 10י 40מ 400ת   200ר 50נ

בְּשֶׁבֶת
Bih Sheh Beht / In Sabbath
704 = 400ת 2ב 300ש 2ב

In בְּשֶׁבֶת meaning 'In Sabbath' the Letter ב Bet reminds each Jew that on Sabbath we have two souls. In other Words a poured lamp burns brighter. Our revelation is greater. Note even though this is an Observance for the Priests, i.e. to keep the Lamp burning continually the Command was specifically given to The People of Israel.

Exodus 27.20
And you shall Command Everything from the Letter Aleph to the Letter Tav of The People of Israel...

This informs us that there is more to this Observance. Most Jews are not the Kohanim / Priests so why give this charge to us who cannot enter or serve in the Mishkon or the Bet Ha Mikdosh? We are to serve. Our service is within our own individual Mishkon. Our service is to the Temples of B'nei Noach. We are their priests. It is our responsibility to keep their lamp burning.

Parshat Shemot Ki TeeSaw

Exodus 30:11 - 34.35

What Is Man's Atonement?

Dear Ones, in Parshat Ki Tisa like many other places within the Torah we zoom in on Observances given to the People of Israel. We will examine two. First we Observe that the Atonement for man is Ha Torah, i.e. the 613 Observances of Ha Torah.

Shemot 30.11,12

וַיְדַבֵּר יְהֹוָה אֶל־מֹשֶׁה לֵּאמֹר :
כִּי תִשָּׂא אֶת־רֹאשׁ בְּנֵי־יִשְׂרָאֵל לִפְקֻדֵיהֶם וְנָתְנוּ **אִישׁ כֹּפֶר**
נַפְשׁוֹ לַיהֹוָה בִּפְקֹד אֹתָם וְלֹא־יִהְיֶה בָהֶם נֶגֶף בִּפְקֹד אֹתָם:

Exodus 30.11.12
And He, The Lord Spoke To Moshe to say, When you take everything from Aleph to Tav of the head count of the People of Israel **to**

determine their numbers **each man will give an atonement pledge** *for his soul to The Lord when you count them. There will be no plague among the when you count them.*

אִישׁ כֹּפֶר
Eesh - Koh-Pehr / Each Man's Atonement
611 = 200ר 80פ 20כ   300ש 10י 1א

תּוֹרָה
Torah
611 = 5ה 200ר 6ו 400ת

בְּנֵי־יִשְׂרָאֵל
B'nai Yisroel / People of Israel
603 = 30ל 1א 200ר 300ש 10י   10י 50נ 2ב
611 = 603 + 8 Letters

The Mispar Musaphi [The number of Letters are added to the Gematria of the Word]. Rabbi Gutman G. Locks The Spice Of Torah Gematria (Judaica Press New York N.Y. Judaica Press 1985) p XXII

Shemot 31.12-17

וַיֹּאמֶר יְהֹוָה אֶל־מֹשֶׁה לֵּאמֹר: וְאַתָּה דַּבֵּר אֶל־בְּנֵי יִשְׂרָאֵל לֵאמֹר אַךְ אֶת־שַׁבְּתֹתַי תִּשְׁמֹרוּ כִּי אוֹת הִוא בֵּינִי וּבֵינֵיכֶם לְדֹרֹתֵיכֶם לָדַעַת כִּי אֲנִי יְהֹוָה מְקַדִּשְׁכֶם: וּשְׁמַרְתֶּם אֶת־הַשַּׁבָּת כִּי קֹדֶשׁ הִוא לָכֶם מְחַלְלֶיהָ מוֹת יוּמָת כִּי כָּל־הָעֹשֶׂה בָה מְלָאכָה וְנִכְרְתָה הַנֶּפֶשׁ הַהִוא מִקֶּרֶב עַמֶּיהָ: שֵׁשֶׁת יָמִים יֵעָשֶׂה מְלָאכָה וּבַיּוֹם הַשְּׁבִיעִי שַׁבַּת שַׁבָּתוֹן קֹדֶשׁ לַיהֹוָה כָּל־הָעֹשֶׂה מְלָאכָה בְּיוֹם הַשַּׁבָּת מוֹת יוּמָת: וְשָׁמְרוּ בְנֵי־יִשְׂרָאֵל אֶת־הַשַּׁבָּת לַעֲשׂוֹת אֶת־הַשַּׁבָּת לְדֹרֹתָם בְּרִית עוֹלָם:

Exodus 31. 12-17

And the Lord Spoke to Moshe, Saying, Speak you also to the people of Israel, saying, Truly My Sabbaths you shall keep; for it is a sign between Me and you throughout your generations; that you may know that I am the Lord that does sanctify you. You shall keep the Sabbath therefore; for it is Holy to you; every one who defiles it shall surely be put to death; for whoever does any work in it, that soul shall be cut off from among his people. Six days may work be done; but in the seventh is the Sabbath of rest, Holy to the Lord; whoever does any work in the Sabbath Day, he shall surely be put to death. Therefore the people of Israel shall keep the Sabbath, to observe the Sabbath throughout their generations, for an everlasting covenant. It is a sign between me and the people of Israel forever; for in six days the Lord Made Heaven and earth, and on the Seventh Day He Rested, and was Refreshed.

There are misunderstandings about Sabbath Observance. Why? Most non-Jews do not understand that Sabbath Observance is a Command given ONLY to The People of Israel. We the People of Israel MUST Observe the Sabbath. The rest of the world does not have to Observe our Sabbath. There are some non-Jews who disagree with Ha Torah's instructions regarding Sabbath Observance...

Many non-Jews do not understand the meaning of B'nei Yisroel... Maybe some do not care. Maybe some disagree with Ha Torah's explicit instructions regarding who B'nei Yisroel is...

So this results in non-Jews attempting to redefine Sabbath Observance and Ha Torah's definition of B'nei Yisroel.

Dear Ones... We cannot alter the meaning of Ha Torah like this. Ha Torah's definition of Sabbath Observance and B'nei Yisroel must remain exactly the same as the day The Lord Gave it. The definition of Sabbath Observance and B'nei Yisroel cannot adapt to new meanings **PERIOD!** Their definition and purpose remain the same from generation to generation. We MUST honor the original definition of Sabbath Observance and B'nei Yisroel. There can be no variance from this!!

In accordance with the above verses, Sabbath Observance is given and required ONLY of B'nei Yisroel. What does this mean? Sabbath Observance is given only to the descendants of Yisroel / Yaakov and those who convert to Judaism. These are the descendants who have passed down proper Sabbath Observance from generation to generation.

It is possible that one may be of Jewish descent yet not be included in the Torah's meaning of B'nei Yisroel. How can this be?

When Jews violate the Torah by intermarriage with non-Jews, immediately Sabbath Observance is affected. The marriage is not recognized by God, the Giver of Ha Torah. Since the marriage is not recognized by God, other areas are also not recognized.

Less observant Jews may disagree with Ha Torah's requirement that Jews marry Jews. Why? Some Jews do not understand why Jews are required to marry Jews. For one reason or another Torah Observance was not handed down to them by parents or relatives. Maybe their parents belonged to that group who considered themselves JEWISH FREE THINKERS.

Jewish parents that drift away from Torah Observance will not pass along many Torah Observances to their children and may have even encouraged them to marry outside of Judaism.

Their parents or grandparents may have begun observing other religions. The children were not raised to understand or how to Observe Ha Torah.

SOME parents or grandparents were forced to earn a living by working on Sabbath... Working on Sabbath led to other Torah breakdowns. As a result the children are raised with redefined Torah Observances...

Distant relatives may have been forced to join another religion. Over a period of time Torah Observances were overrun or confused by teachings of other religions...

Some who are not Jewish want to observe the Hebrew Scriptures like Jews do...

Some Jews and non Jews who are Christian / Messianic believe they are in-grafted into the house of Israel. They believe they are Jewish through the blood of Jesus....

Holy Readers, we could go on and on with

different forms of Jewish Assimilation and non-Jewish beliefs... It is very possible that ONE IS THE VICTIM OF JEWISH ASSIMILATION! It is also very possible that one is the VICTIM OF FALSE TEACHINGS regarding Sabbath Observance or B'nei Yisroel. One is the product of what someone else did!! Now one finds themselves here reading this discussion yet, you have done nothing. Your Jewish past is not recognized for one reason or another. You have only accepted what someone else taught you. You feel this incredible need to return to The God of Avraham, Yitzchok and Yaakov but find more doors closed than open. You receive much rejection and little or no encouragement. In some situations you are looked down on. You may feel like dirt. It can even be worse.

Only The Lord Knows our heart. Only The Lord Knows our intention. Only The Lord Knows our desires. Only The Lord Knows and understands our past, present and future. Ha Torah requires Jews to be extremely careful with those not defined as B'nei Yisroel. One's commitment to Torah Judaism CANNOT BE A FAD! One's commitment to Torah Judaism has to be very real. Rabbis are frequently inundated with those who T H I N K... they have Jewish relatives... with those who feel Jewish... with those who are deceptive... etc., etc., etc.

Dear Ones, you may think that you want to be Jewish... that you want to return to the religion of your distant relatives... AND this may be true, but there is much more to being an Observant Jew than just a whimsical desire or even a very extremely sincere desire. To return to Judaism requires much!! To convert to Judaism requires at least two years of dedicated study. There is much to being a descendant of B'nei Yisroel.

In this we see the actual definition of 'B'nei Yisroel' as those descendants of Yaakov who observe Torah in Words and in Letters...

The words B'nei Yisroel are found only seven times in the Book of Creation, Bereishis / Genesis.

Within the Letters of B'nei Yisroel we find:

Aleph for Avraham
Yud for Yitzchok
Yud for Yaakov

Shin for Sarah
Lamid for Leah
Reish for Rivkah
Reish for Rachel

Parshat Shemot Vayakhel

Exodus 35.1 - 38.20

Why Was The Altar Made?

Dear Ones, within the first six Words of Shemot 38.1 is a special message, an acronym formed from the first Letter of each Word.

Shemot 38.1

וַיַּעַשׂ אֶת־מִזְבַּח הָעֹלָה עֲצֵי שִׁטִּים חָמֵשׁ אַמּוֹת אָרְכּוֹ וְחָמֵשׁ־אַמּוֹת רָחְבּוֹ רָבוּעַ וְשָׁלֹשׁ אַמּוֹת קֹמָתוֹ:

וַיַּעַשׂ אֶת־מִזְבַּח הָעֹלָה עֲצֵי שִׁטִּים

Hebrew is a unique language. Letters are added and removed from the root Word. Let's examine this. A Word may have many different spellings. An example of this is the first Word in Genesis 38.1. Two Letters are added to the front of first word וַיַּעַשׂ Vah Yah Ahs and one Letter is removed. וַיַּעַשׂ Vah Yah Ahs is normally spelled עשה. Here in Genesis 38.1 the Letters ו Vav and י Yud are added to the beginning of the Word and the Letter Hey is removed from the conclusion of the Word. The Letters ע Ayin and שׁ Sin are the root Letters. The Vav means 'and'. The Vav is a connecting Letter when it appears at the beginning of a Word. All but several Verses in Genesis begin with the Letter Vav. This Teaches us how each Verse is connected to the next Verse. In וַיַּעַשׂ Vah Yah Ahs the י Yud which follows the Vav means 'he'. When Letters are added and removed this changes the Gematria of the Word. Also It can be challenging to know which Letters are added and which are removed from the original Word. So the beginning Letter in וַיַּעַשׂ Vah Yah Ahs is actually the ע Ayin which is the third Letter from the right.

Sometimes Words are added or attached to the front of the Word that follows as in the second and third Words of Genesis 38.1. Notice the Word אֶת Eht. Many Teach that the Word Eht does not have a meaning. Some Teach that the Eht is a direct article for the Word that follows. At

B'nai Noach Torah Institute LLC we Teach that the Word Eht has a very special meaning that is frequently used throughout Ha Torah. We Teach that the first Letter Aleph represents the first Letter of the Hebrew Aleph Bet (Alphabet) and that the Letter Tav represents the last Letter of the Hebrew Aleph Bet. When they are employed as the Word אֶת Eht this takes on a very special meaning. We Teach this means 'everything from the first Letter Aleph to the last Letter Tav. So when Ha Torah Says that God Created the Heavens and the Earth we include the meaning of the אֶת Eht.

Bereisheit 1.1

בְּרֵאשִׁית בָּרָא אֱלֹהִים אֵת הַשָּׁמַיִם וְאֵת הָאָרֶץ:

Genesis 1.1
In the beginning God Created everything from Aleph to Tav of the Heavens and everything from Aleph to Tav of the earth.

Here the Word אֶת Eht represents that God Created everything in the heavens and everything in the earth. Nothing is excluded. God

Created it all.

אֵת הַשָּׁמַיִם
everything from Aleph to Tav of the Heavens

וְאֵת הָאָרֶץ
everything from Aleph to Tav of the earth

Rabbi Akiba, Says that the very fact that Eht contains the Alef Tav implies that it superimposes the entire alphabet between the subject verb and the predicated noun adding all things that pertain to that noun Aryeh Kaplan The Bahir (Lanham, Maryland, Rowman & Littlefield Publishers) 1st edition, 2004 p xxii • Mysterious Signs Of The Torah Revealed In Exodus Dr. Akiva Gamliel Belk, p 48

Exodus 38.1

'And He made everything from Aleph to Tav of the Altar of offering...' Even though the Holy Altar is man made it was made at the direction of the Lord God through Moshe.

Exodus 35.1

And Moses gathered all the congregation of the people of Israel together, and said to them, These are the Words which the Lord Has Commanded, that you should do them.

Exodus 35.4

And Moses spoke to all the congregation of the people of Israel, saying, This is the Word that the Lord Commanded, Saying...

Exodus 35.10

And every wise hearted among you shall come, and make Everything from Aleph to Tav of all that the Lord Has Commanded;

Exodus 35.11 - 19

Everything from Aleph to Tav of The Tabernacle, Everything from Aleph to Tav of Its tent, and Everything from Aleph to Tav of Its Covering, Everything from Aleph to Tav of Its Clasps, and Everything from Aleph to

Tav of The Its Boards, Everything from Aleph to Tav of Its Bars, Everything from Aleph to Tav of Its Pillars, and Everything from Aleph to Tav of Its Sockets, Everything from Aleph to Tav of The Ark, and Everything from Aleph to Tav of Its Poles, Everything from Aleph to Tav of The Covering, and Everything from Aleph to Tav of The Veil of the screen, Everything from Aleph to Tav of The Table, and Everything from Aleph to Tav of Its Poles, and Everything from Aleph to Tav of all Its Utensils, and Everything from Aleph to Tav of The Bread of display. Everything from Aleph to Tav of The Menorah for the Light, and Everything from Aleph to Tav of The Its Furniture, and Everything from Aleph to Tav of The Its lamps, with the oil for the light, And Everything from Aleph to Tav of The Incense altar, and Everything from Aleph to Tav of The Its Poles, and Everything from Aleph to Tav of The Anointing Oil, and Everything from Aleph to Tav of The Incense of Spices, and Everything from Aleph to Tav of The Screen for the door at the entrance of

The Tabernacle, Everything from Aleph to Tav of The Altar of Burnt Offering, with Everything from Aleph to Tav of Its Bronze Grating, Everything from Aleph to Tav of Its Poles, and Everything from Aleph to Tav of The all its Utensils, Everything from Aleph to Tav of The Basin and Everything from Aleph to Tav of The Its Pedestal, Everything from Aleph to Tav of The Curtains of the court, Everything from Aleph to Tav of The Its Pillars, and Everything from Aleph to Tav of Their Sockets, and Everything from Aleph to Tav of The Screen for the door of the Court, Everything from Aleph to Tav of The Pegs of The Tabernacle, and Everything from Aleph to Tav of The Pegs of the Court, and Everything from Aleph to Tav of Their Cords, Everything from Aleph to Tav of The Cloths, for the Holy Articles, Everything from Aleph to Tav of The Holy Garments for Aaron the Priest, and Everything from Aleph to Tav of The Garments of his Sons, to Minister in the Priest's Office.

We have just experienced the Word אֶת Eht 42 times. The Message is repeated over and over.

Everything The Lord God Says is important. How important is it when The Lord God Repeats אֶת Eht 42 times over ten Verses in Ha Torah? Here the Word אֶת Eht is impressed on us so we had better sit up and pay attention!!

Each of the 42 times אֶת Eht proceeds the Word that it is referencing. It is very clear that The Lord God Emphasized every detail of the making of The Holy Tabernacle. When we read אֶת־מִזְבַּח Eht - Meez Bah Ach we realize the emphasis is on the Altar and not on Eht. The Eht is placing the emphasis on Altar. Therefore the Eht even though it is one of the six Words of the acronym we will be reviewing we will not include Eht in the acronym.

It is not by chance that the Eht occurs 42 times among these passages. Our Sages Teach us that our Creator has a forty-two Letter Name. Sanhedrin 60a The Zohar Teaches that the 'Engraven ineffable Name is formed of the forty-two letters of the work of creation.' Zohar B 223b

Having said this we will now examine the acronym.

ע Ayin = וַיַּעַשׂ

מ Mem = מִזְבַּח

עַם Ahm means 'Nation'

עַם Ahm means 'Relative / Kinsman'

It is through the making of the Altar, i.e. It is though making use of the Altar that we become a relative, that we have a relationship with The Lord God.

The Letter ה Hey is an introductory Letter that means 'The'. The ה Hey is added on to the front of the Word Oh Law meaning to rise upward into the Heavens. So it becomes הָעֹלָה Haw Oh Law meaning 'The fragrance that rises from a burnt offering up into the Heavens.' In הָעֹלָה Haw Oh Law the root Word begins with the second Letter, i.e. the ע Ayin.

So it is like Mystically the acronym of the first four Words is Saying 'the nation from seventy'. What does this mean?

Genesis 46.27

And the sons of Joseph, who were born to him in Egypt, were two souls; **all the souls of the house of Jacob, who came to Egypt, were seventy.**

עֲצֵי שִׁטִים

The last Two Words spell עש which is again is Mystically a reflection of 'to make'. However it is much more than just to make.

ע Ayin = עֲצֵי meaning tree.
ש Sin = שִׁטִים See Teem meaning acacia

So Mystically, the acronym of the first six Words is Saying 'the nation from seventy shall make'. 'The Kinsmen [of The Lord God] shall make? What shall we make? פת Poht - meaning an opening or meaning a morsel of bread. We shall make an opening for the world to know The Lord God. We shall make it possible that even if one brings just a morsel of bread, i.e a little flour mixed with water and places it upon the Holy Altar for the Fragrance to rise that offering will be accepted by The Lord God.

The Gematria of עַם ע עשׁ is 480.

עַם עשׁ

'The Kinsmen [of The Lord God] shall make? What shall we make? פת Poht [480]- An Opening What shall we make? פת Poht - An Altar to receive a morsel of bread [flour and water] for the offering that rises up to The Lord God...

Yisaiah 56.7

וַהֲבִיאוֹתִים אֶל־הַר קָדְשִׁי וְשִׂמַּחְתִּים בְּבֵית תְּפִלָּתִי עוֹלֹתֵיהֶם וְזִבְחֵיהֶם לְרָצוֹן עַל־מִזְבְּחִי כִּי בֵיתִי בֵּית־תְּפִלָּה יִקָּרֵא לְכָל־הָעַמִּים:

Isaiah 56.7

Even them will I bring to My Holy Mountain, and make them joyful in My House of prayer; their burnt offerings and their sacrifices shall be accepted upon My Altar; for My House shall be called a house of prayer for all peoples.

עמ עשה = 480

ע70 מ40 ע70 ע70 ש300 = 480

פת

Opening / Morsel [of Bread]

פ80 ת400 = 480

When we consider all the Letters to the acronym we observe who is given the charge to keep the Holy Altar.

עמ ע עשה

וַיַּעַשׂ אֶת־מִזְבַּח הָעֹלָה עֲצֵי שִׁטִּים

עמ ע עשה = 555

שֹׁמְרֵי

Those who Keep

ש300 מ40 ר200 י10 = 580

BaMidbar 3.28

בְּמִסְפַּר כָּל־זָכָר מִבֶּן־חֹדֶשׁ וָמָעְלָה שְׁמֹנַת אֲלָפִים וְשֵׁשׁ מֵאוֹת **שֹׁמְרֵי** מִשְׁמֶרֶת הַקֹּדֶשׁ:

Numbers 3.28

In the number of all the males, from a month old and upward, were eight thousand and six hundred, keeping the charge of the Holy.

The Altar is Holy. The sacrifices on the Altar are Holy. Our Creator Appointed the Tribe of Levi as guardians of Keeping the Holy Articles.

Devri Torah Parshat Pekudei

Shemot 38.21 - 40.38

Can One Be Entirely Sanctified? ©

Dear Ones, my wife, Rebbetzin Revi was sharing with the Ladies class that we were Created for the purpose of serving The Lord God. In our discussion here I would like for us to examine how we serve our Creator.

Exodus 40.1-8
And The Lord Spoke to Moshe, saying, On the first day of the first month set up the Tabernacle of the Tent of Meeting. And put in it the Ark of the Covenant, and cover the Ark with the Veil. And bring in the Table, and set in order the things that are to be set in order upon it; and bring in the Lamp stands, and light its lamps. And set the altar of gold for the incense before the ark of the

Covenant, and put the screen of the door to the Tabernacle. And set the altar of the burnt offering before the door of the Tabernacle of the Tent of Meeting. And set the basin between the tent of the congregation and the altar, and shall put water in it. And set up the court around it, and hang up the screen at the court gate.

Shemot 40.9

וְלָקַחְתָּ אֶת־שֶׁמֶן הַמִּשְׁחָה וּמָשַׁחְתָּ אֶת־הַמִּשְׁכָּן וְאֶת־כָּל־אֲשֶׁר־בּוֹ וְקִדַּשְׁתָּ אֹתוֹ וְאֶת־כָּל־כֵּלָיו וְהָיָה קֹדֶשׁ:

Exodus 40.9

And take everything from Aleph to Tav of the anointing oil, **and anoint** *everything from Aleph to Tav of the tabernacle, and all that goes in it,* **and consecrate them,** *and everything from Aleph to Tav of all its utensils;* **and it shall be Holy / Separated.**

Dear Ones, note the Words, וְאֶת־כָּל־אֲשֶׁר־בּוֹ and all that is in it. Here we learn everything in the Mishkan was anointed.

Note the Words, וְקִדַּשְׁתָּ אֹתוֹ *and consecrate them.* Here we learn everything in the Mishkan was Holy / Separated.

Note the Words, *and it shall be Separated.* Here we learn everything in the Mishkan was וְהָיָה קֹדֶשׁ Holy / Separated. Everything in the Tabernacle is considered as if it were one even though there are many parts.

Moshe was Instructed on what to place in the Mishkan / Tabernacle. He was Instructed where each Holy Article should be placed to serve. In this same way each of us has a place we belong and serve from.

Shemot 40.10

וּמָשַׁחְתָּ אֶת־מִזְבַּח הָעֹלָה וְאֶת־כָּל־כֵּלָיו וְקִדַּשְׁתָּ אֶת־הַמִּזְבֵּחַ וְהָיָה הַמִּזְבֵּחַ קֹדֶשׁ קָדָשִׁים :

Exodus 40.10
And anoint *everything from Aleph to Tav of the Altar of rising up, and everything from Aleph to Tav of All its Utensils,* ***and sanctify***

everything from Aleph to Tav of the Altar; and it shall be an Altar **Holy of the Holiest.**

Dear Ones, note the Words, rising up. Most translations Say burnt Offerings. They translate the Holy Language as Burnt Offerings because Burnt Offerings Rise up. This is the intent but not the translation. The correct translation is rising up. Why is making this distinction important? It is because within us is a Mishkan / a Temple. And within our Temple is an Altar that does not offer Burnt Offerings. Yet the Temple within us has the ability to rise up.

We must inquire about the Word וְקִדַּשְׁתָּ Vih Kee Dah Shi Taw meaning to be Holy... to be Separated... to be Sanctified... What has the ability within us to rise up and to be Holy... to be Separated... to be Sanctified... It is what proceeds from our lips. The Gematria of וְקִדַּשְׁתָּ Vih Kee Dah shi Taw is 810. The Gematria of שְׂפָתֶיךָ Sah Faw Teh Kaw meaning, your lips is 810. When we place these two Words together they say וְקִדַּשְׁתָּ שְׂפָתֶיךָ *'And you shall Sanctify your lips.'* In the morning before we pray

Shemoneh Esrei we say, O Lord Open my lips that my mouth may say / declare Your Praise.

We say the same Words *O Lord Open my lips that my mouth may say / declare Your Praise,* at Minchah / afternoon prayers and at Maariv/ evening prayers and at Mussaf on Sabbath and High Holy Days. Why?

There is a mystical relationship between Holiness between Sanctification between Separation and our lips. As you know every Letter in the original language has a numerical equivalence. We see this relationship in the total of each of these Words.

The four Words that we will study the Gematria of each have the Letter Shin / Sin. Normally I write the three arms of the Letter Shin / Sin without noting the direction that the top of each arm faces. Because of this one who studies with me will not see the three directions of each arm of the Letter Shin / Sin. Don't be fooled just because I use a more simple block style. If you examines the block style of others they will notice the three direction of the arms of the Letter 'Shin / Sin. Rabbi Michael L. Munk, author of The Wisdom in The Hebrew Alphabet has many examples of what I am referring to. He Says that The Letter Shin / Sin is the symbol of Divine Power and Script - but also of Corruption. Rabbi Michael Munk The Wisdom In The Hebrew Alphabet Mesorah Publications, Brooklyn, N.Y. 1990), p 207

When one observes the directions of the arms they are facing each other and that explains how the meaning of The Letter Shin / Sin has two extremes within It's definition, i.e. Divine Power and Script - but also of Corruption. We know that Divine Power or Script is not corrupt. How Rabbi Munk states that the Letter Shin represents corruption. So within the Letter Shin we have the Yetzer Tov and Yetzer Raw. When we look at the four words we realize that the Letter Shin Mystically has the potential to take us closer to the Observances or away from the Observances. We also notice that Righteous will be tested because the Letter Shin / Sin is part of Holiness / Separation as is the Moshiach / Messiah.

וְקִדַּשְׁתָּ Vih Kee Dah Shi Taw
meaning to be Holy… to be Separated… to be Sanctified…
810 = 400ת 300ש 4ד 100ק 6ו

שְׂפָתֶיךָ Sah Faw Theh Kaw
meaning, your lips
810 = 20ך 10י 400ת 80פ 300ש

Dear Ones, Mystically this Teaches us that our place is to let Holy Words flow from the Temple within us. This also Teaches us that when one says words that are not Holy… Sanctified… Carefully thought out words they are out of their place… They are out of the anointed Mishkan… They are out of the anointed Temple… This is noted in the Gematria 754 of the Word וּמָשַׁחְתָּ Ooh Maw Shahch Taw meaning *and anoint [with oil]*. It is also noted in the Gematria 754 of the Word וְשָׂמַחְתָּ Vih Saw Mahch Taw meaning *and you shall rejoice.* Simply put when one is anointed it brings about rejoicing. Again, We see this relationship in the total of each of these Words.

וּמָשַׁחְתָּ Ooh Maw Shahch Taw
meaning *and anoint [with oil]*
6 ו 40 מ 300 ש 8 ח 400 ת = 754

וְשָׂמַחְתָּ Vih Saw Mahch Taw
meaning *and you shall rejoice*
6 ו 400 ת 8 ח 40 מ 300 ש = 754

Dear Ones, Mystically this Teaches us that our place should be one of rejoicing. Notice that people who rejoice have a special place of anointing. Even though they may not be the the Ark, or the Table or the Lamp Stands or the Veil or the Altar their Spirit was in the Holy Mishkan when it was anointed. They sing forth praise and rejoice in their Creator even though they were not selected to be one of these important pieces to serve in the Holy Temple.

Shemot 40.11

וּמָשַׁחְתָּ אֶת־הַכִּיֹּר וְאֶת־כַּנּוֹ וְקִדַּשְׁתָּ
אֹתוֹ :

Exodus 40.11
And anoint everything from Aleph to Tav of

the basin and everything from Aleph to Tav of its pedestal, **and sanctify it.**

Shemot 40.12

וְהִקְרַבְתָּ אֶת־אַהֲרֹן וְאֶת־בָּנָיו אֶל־פֶּתַח אֹהֶל מוֹעֵד וְרָחַצְתָּ אֹתָם בַּמָּיִם :

Exodus 40.12

And you shall bring everything from Aleph to Tav of Aaron and everything from Aleph to Tav of his sons to the door of the Tent of Meeting, and wash them with water.

Shemot 40.13

וְהִלְבַּשְׁתָּ אֶת־אַהֲרֹן אֵת בִּגְדֵי הַקֹּדֶשׁ וּמָשַׁחְתָּ אֹתוֹ וְקִדַּשְׁתָּ אֹתוֹ וְכִהֵן לִי :

Exodus 40.13

And you shall dress everything from Aleph to Tav of Aaron in the Holy Garments, **and anoint him, and sanctify him** to Me a Priest.

Dear Ones, what does Isaiah 61.3 say?

To appoint to those who mourn in Zion, to give to

them a garland instead of ashes, the oil of joy instead of mourning, the garment of praise instead of the spirit of heaviness; that they might be called trees of righteousness, the planting of the Lord, that he might be glorified.

Shemot 40.14

וְאֶת־בָּנָיו תַּקְרִיב וְהִלְבַּשְׁתָּ אֹתָם כֻּתֳּנֹת ׃

Exodus 40.14
And everything from Aleph to Tav of his sons, bring near and dress them with coats;

Shemot 40.15

וּמָשַׁחְתָּ אֹתָם כַּאֲשֶׁר מָשַׁחְתָּ אֶת־אֲבִיהֶם וְכִהֲנוּ לִי וְהָיְתָה לִהְיֹת לָהֶם מָשְׁחָתָם לִכְהֻנַּת עוֹלָם לְדֹרֹתָם ׃

Exodus 40.15
*And anoint them, everything from Aleph to Tav of like that **anointing** of their father, and Priest's to Me for their **anointing** as Priests is **everlasting** for generations.*

Shemot 40.16

וַיַּעַשׂ מֹשֶׁה כְּכֹל אֲשֶׁר צִוָּה יְהֹוָה אֹתוֹ כֵּן עָשָׂה :

Exodus 40.16
And Moshe did according to all like HaShem Commanded him, so did he.

Dear Ones, who was anointed? Who is the Moshiach / Messiah? The Moshiach was Aharon and each of his sons. Aharon and his sons were entirely sanctified. They were separated and anointed. Yet, we who are not anointed can live sanctified lives. We can live lives that are separated to the Lord. Aharon and his sons, i.e. the Priests would be supported by communal offerings. They worked in the area of the Holy Tabernacle. They lived close to the Holy Tabernacle. The Creator Established a society in and around the Holy Mishkon / Holy Tabernacle that was conducive to Holiness / Separation. We who are not the priests lack these important supports to the Holy Way of Living. We are not separated and anointed to work in and around the Holy Tabernacle. We may not have communal support. We may even live outside of the Jewish community. Note that each step is farther away from were we desire to be. Yet it is possible to be Holy / Separated!!

May The Lord Bless all who Observe Torah Mitzvot and for those who try.

Blessings and peace,

Dr. Akiva Gamliel and Rebbetzin Revi

Chazak - חזק

Gematria Chart

Aleph	א	1			
Bet	ב	2			
Gimmel	ג	3			
Dalet	ד	4			
Hey	ה	5			
Vav	ו	6			
Zayin	ז	7			
Chet	ח	8			
Tet	ט	9			
Yud	י	10			
Chof	כ	20	Final	ך	500
Lamid	ל	30			
Mem	מ	40	Final	ם	600
Nun	נ	50	Final	ן	700
Samech	ס	60			
Ayin	ע	70			
Pey	פ	80	Final	ף	800
Tzzadi	צ	90		ץ	900
Quf	ק	100			
Reish	ר	200			
Shin	ש	300			
Tav	ת	400			

SCRIPTURE INDEX

Genesis	Page	Exodus	Page
1.1	80, 117	1.5	60
1.2	75	2.11, 12	68, 69
1.4	79	4.22	21
1.14	79	4.23	22
2.16	77	6.7	43
3.14	73	7.5	44
10.3	54	7.17	31, 39, 42
12.1 - 3	85, 86	8.6	31, 39, 43
15.1	84	8.18	31, 40, 43
15.14	54	9.16	44
18.2	71	9.29	32, 40, 43
24.67	32, 33	10.21	47, 50, 52
38.1	115, 116	10.22	49, 51, 52
45.27	36	10.22, 23	53
46.27	60, 124	13.17, 18	59

Exodus	Page	Exodus	Page
14.19,20	55	31.12 - 17	107
15	62	35.1	119
15.1	63	35.4	119
15.11	24	35.10	119
15.21	64	35.11 - 19	119
15.18	24	38.1	115, 116
18.21	76	38.1	118
19.6	22	40.1 - 8	128
21.1	83	40.9	130
21.12	70	40.10	131
24.1	60	40.11	136
25.1	91	40.12	137
25.2	91	40.13	137
25.3	94	40.14	138
27.20	97, 102	40.15	138
30.11, 12	105	40.16	139

Leviticus	Page	Psalms	Pages
11.45	27	119.105	54
20.10	70	145.21	24, 25
		Isaiah	Page
Numbers	**Page**	56.7	125
3.28	126, 127	60.2 - 5	55
		61.3	135
Deut.	**Page**	145.21	24, 25
7.6 - 11	87		
14.23	40, 41	**Job**	**Page**
18.9	41	10.22	
Psalms	**Pages**		
18.12	49		
27	55		
51.17	24		
100.4	25		
105.1 - 10	88		

GEMATRIA INDEX

Gematria	Page	Gematria	Page
5	60	120	61
15	60	130	78
18	58	226	85
22	36	234	86
23	38	243	85
40	61, 93	292	86
42	84, 121	345	61
42	122	360	51
48	73	400	26
52	79	401	38
57	85	420	74, 75, 80
70	123	421	36
100	57	424	37
110	92	430	84
112	98	474	32, 40, 41
115	62		

Gematria	Page	Gematria	Page
474	42	1000	80
480	124, 125	1130	48
484	84	6000	80
501	92, 99, 100		
516	63		
526	84, 85, 86		
526	87		
555	126		
580	126		
603	106		
611	92, 106		
613	28, 104		
704	102		
754	135, 136		
810	130, 132		
810	135		
835	23		

About The Author

Dr. Akiva Gamliel Belk

Jewish, Husband, Father,
Grandfather and Step Great Grandfather.

Graduate:
A.A. Long Beach City College,
B.A. Southern California Bible College,
M.A. Southern California Theological Seminary,
D. Th. Southern California Theological Seminary,
D. Th. Denver Charismatic Theological Seminary

Individual Study:
Rabbi Dovid Nusbaum,
Bais Medrash at Yeshiva Toras Chaim,
Hornosteipler Rebbe, Mordicai Tewerski
Group Study:
Rabbi Yaakov Meyer, Aish Denver
Rabbi Yisroel Engel, Director, Colorado Chabad.

Founder:
Jewishpath.org
Jewishlink.net
7commands.com
Bnti.us

Dean of Jewish Studies
B'nai Noach Torah Institute, LLC
Biblical Online Studies

http://www.jewishpath.org
http://www.bnti.us

Author of various books.
bnti.us/books.html

Businessman:
Realtor and Property Investor

Books By Dr. Akiva Gamliel

SERIES OF BOOKS

Gematria And Mysticism - Series

Gematria And Mysticism IN GENESIS - Book I
This book is the first in a series of five books. Book 1 covers Genesis Chapters 1 through 10. In this series of books the reader will be introduced to truths not discussed among the religions of the world. Hebrew in the Bible unveils answers to many mysteries. The entire Bible is founded upon Genesis, Exodus, Leviticus, Numbers and Deuteronomy and the truths that flow out of these five books is different than the rest of the Bible. Why? There is a system of Hebrew Letters with which each have a numerical value that have the power to reveal interesting and mystifying relationships within the Hebrew Letters, Words, Phrases etc. of the First Five Books. The cost of this book is a small investment for what the reader will learn.

Gematria And Mysticism IN GENESIS - Book II
This book is the second in a series of five books. Book 2 is a continues where Book 1 concluded. Book 2 covers Genesis Chapters 11 through 20. As in the first book the reader will be introduced to truths not discussed among the religions of the world. Hebrew in the Bible unveils answers to many mysteries. The entire Bible is founded upon Genesis, Exodus, Leviticus, Numbers and Deuteronomy and the truths that flow out of these five books is different than the rest of the Bible. Why? There is a system of Hebrew Letters with which each have a numerical value that have the power to reveal interesting and mystifying relationships within the Hebrew Letters, Words, Phrases etc. of the First Five Books. The cost of this book is a small investment for what the reader will learn.

Mysterious SIGNS Of The Torah - Series

Mysterious SIGNS Of The Torah in GENESIS
This book is the first in a series of five books.

Mysterious SIGNS Of The Torah Revealed In GENESIS is an exploration of Biblical truths organized into the Weekly Parshat study of the Bible. Dr. Akiva Gamliel has been recording and referencing decades of study and research. He has gathered, compiled and organized years of discovery into this mystical book for us to learn, enjoy and share. Many years can pass between one discovery to another which forms a bridge between two discoveries. Revelations are the product of many bridges. Enclosed in this book are some of these special relationships.

Mysterious SIGNS Of The Torah in EXODUS
This is the second in a series of Five Books, God Willing. This book is deep, intense, inspiring and extremely interesting. Yet, it is easy to read and follow. Dr. Akiva Gamliel includes a Gematria Chart in the beginning of the book. Like each of Dr. Akiva Gamliel's Gematria books there are special Gematrias waiting for the Reader to discover. There is a special sweetness in sharing a Torah Gematria / Sign during a wonderful warm Friday evening Sabbath meal or on another occasion.

Mysterious SIGNS Of The Torah in LEVITICUS
This is the third in a series of Five Books, God Willing. This book is deep, intense, inspiring and extremely interesting. Yet, it is easy to read and follow. Dr. Akiva Gamliel includes a Gematria Chart in the beginning of the book . Like each of Dr. Akiva Gamliel's Gematria books there are special Gematrias waiting for the Reader to discover. There is a special sweetness in sharing a Torah Gematria / Sign during a wonderful warm Friday evening Sabbath meal or on another occasion.

A Taste Of Torah - Series

Gematria Azer -
A Taste Of Torah From Genesis
This book is the first in a series of five books. Each Chapter follows the Weekly Parshat with a Torah question, a Gematria or two and a brief discussion. For those that desire each lesson has a matching Video by Dr. Akiva Gamliel Belk, Dean of Jewish Studies at B'nai Noach Torah

Institute, LLC.

Gematria Azer -
A Taste Of Torah From Exodus

This book is the second in a series of five books. Each Chapter follows the Weekly Parshat with a Torah question, a Gematria or two and a brief discussion. For those that desire each lesson has a matching Video by Dr. Akiva Gamliel Belk, Dean of Jewish Studies at B'nai Noach Torah Institute, LLC.

A Sincere Journey Ends Without Jesus

This is an autobiography of my spiritual journey. My journey did not begin with the goal of returning to Judaism. My journey began with a desire to give my Baptist Congregation a historical view of Jesus last six days on earth. My journey has been very challenging for me. If you read this book and if you walk in my footprints believing in Jesus will become a challenge for you also. The difference is I am on this side of the journey now. I have returned to Judaism. The journey of my life can be of great help to you if you discern there are problems with the story the New Testament story of Jesus.

PASSOVER –
The LAST SIX DAYS of Jesus Life On Earth

The Gospel Writers each offer a different perspective of Jesus last six days on Earth. They differ some. I offer my own perspective as a Jew that has been on both sides of this discussion. If you are a Christian... If you believe in Jesus this book will be very challenging. I started on this Journey almost 30 years ago with a desire to give my Baptist Congregation a historical view of Jesus last six days on earth. Since then I have returned to Judaism. I share some of the untold stories and fill in some of the blank pages... My journey can be of great help to you if you discern there are problems with the story the story the Christian Writers tell of Jesus last six days on earth.

Would You Like To Be Jewish ?
This book is the first in a series of three books. Many readers would like to know what it is like to be Jewish. Some have tried to learn what it is like to be Jewish. Some visited with a Rabbi who may have said, something like this, 'Why do you want to convert? Why do you want to be Jewish? We don't do conversions in Judaism.' You ended up walking away disappointed, angered, exasperated, annoyed and very dissatisfied. This book answers questions about what Jewish believe in a way you will not forget.

Would You Like To Be Jewish 2 ?
This book is the second in a series of three books. This is a continuation of the first book, Would You Like To Be Jewish. In this book we learn that God has always had a plan, even before the beginning of Creation. We learn how God Teaches us to repent when we fail and when we make mistakes. We discover God is very understanding, compassionate and forgiving. We share about fallen angels, Satan, hell and how to live eternally with God.

Eve Of Creation RESTORED

Good people make bad mistakes. We are at times careless instead of cautious. We hurt those we love. We become angry for no apparent reason and tense without a trigger. We feel frustration! It feels like life has dealt us a loosing hand. We need a new life. We think, what would it be like to have a new life? We day dream of a place and a time that is different than where we are... We feel like we are on an endless downward spiral. It feels like, if there were any hope, it is a great distance away... We are unhappy with our relationship... relationships... our employment... our earning capacity... our children... It's like everything around us smells!

What do we do? How do we face our endless, whatever? How do we put a stop to our seemingly endless downward spiral? The answer is simple. We repair and restore our image of Eve of Creation. Ha Torah Reveals through HOLY Numbers and Letters how to reverse improper behaviors and IMPROVE our selves.

The Biblical Historical Calendar Book

The Biblical Historical Calendar Book covers

many goals for all walks of life. My calender is a religious calendar and a compilation of many prized wild life photographs including trophy Mule Deer, Elk, Rocky Mountain Goats, Coyotes and Foxes and beautiful birds.

The Biblical Historical Calendar Book focuses on the History of the Bible and the beauty of nature. There is a great deal to learn about the Bible's Calendar while at the same time enjoying some breath taking wildlife photographs. This book provide the readers with interesting information about the measurement of time in the Bible and more than a dozen photographs from my prized nature and wildlife photograph collection. Doors open to many special journeys. Walk in the paths of Noah, Abraham and Moses. Learn how today's calendar is much different from the Biblical Calendar. Why the Biblical calendar changed? How that has impacted us.
We will take an adventure with Noah on the ark. We will follow the Children of Israel out of Egypt to Mount Sinai where The Lord Gave us the Commandments. This is a book that every household can and will enjoy for years to come.

This is an investment that will pay dividends the rest of your life. The Biblical Historical Calendar Book is a precious tool that offers each of us many dates of spirituality and celebration. I wish you much pleasure and enjoyment as you travel through the history of the Bible.

Order Additional Books At:

http://www.bnti.us/books.html

www.ingramcontent.com/pod-product-compliance
Lightning Source LLC
Chambersburg PA
CBHW071720090426
42738CB00009B/1825